Explorin

East Anglia

by bus pass

©Will Black Photography

St. Mary's, Langham in Suffolk - just a half-mile walk from Hunston, on bus route 337 from Bury to Stanton.

Pip Wright

Other books by Pip Wright

Exploring Suffolk by Bus Pass
The Watery Places of Suffolk
Daniel Malden
Lydia
Death Recorded
I Read it in the Local Rag (pub. by Poppyland Publishing)
Thomas Slappe's Booke of Physicke
A Picture History of Margaret Catchpole

Books by Pip & Joy Wright
The Amazing Story of John Heigham Steggall,
'The Suffolk Gipsy'
Newspapers in Suffolk (6 vols)
Grave Reports
Witches in and around Suffolk
Bygone Cotton

See all these at
www.pipwright.com
&
The Diary of a Poor Suffolk Woodman
(with Léonie Robinson, pub. by Poppyland Publishing)
See **www.poppyland.co.uk**

Exploring East Anglia by Bus-Pass
A list of my expeditions

Trips into and beyond Cambridgeshire

Trips across Essex

Trips into Hertfordshire

4

Exploring East Anglia by Bus Pass

When I became sixty in Autumn 2007, I applied for my bus-pass. Pretty soon, I was zooming all over the place and by way of a celebration, by June 2008 had published *'Exploring Suffolk by Bus-Pass'*. Since then, I have continued to use buses, not just as a means of getting from place to place, but by way of creating little adventures. Now our bus-passes permit us to travel well outside our native counties, there are fewer restrictions on our movements and wider horizons beckon.

I am aware that I am lucky to live in Stowmarket, slap-bang in the middle of East Anglia with a host of bus routes running in all directions. People have written to me, complaining that getting back in a day from almost anywhere is difficult if you live in Shimpling or Nedging or South Lopham. To that extent, and to place myself at other starting points, it is true I do sometimes use a car. If a friend is driving to a not-too-distant point, I may ask for a lift and begin my trip from there. Using a bit of imagination, even the odd train or taxi, may offer other opportunities.

Again, however, with this book, all my journeys were under-taken within the daylight hours. Once you start to put timetables together, it is remarkable how far you can travel in a day.

Changes come about from time to time. Just before the publishing of this book, Suffolk announced that they would, from March 2011, implement the 9.30 rule. This means that on weekdays, bus passes will not be able to be used before 9.30 a.m. Some counties have already taken this step. For all that, most of these expeditions could be completed without starting that early.

Suffolk timetables come in a series of small booklets, available from libraries and Tourist Information Offices. Otherwise, you can go to www.suffolkonboard.com or phone 0845 606 6171. Essex put all their timetables together in a book the size of a telephone directory, costing just £1. Cambridgeshire bus routes are fewer, but run more often and for longer. Just two companies cover most of the county, and leaflets for these routes are readily available at Cambridge

Bus Station. Hertfordshire County Council produce booklets for each area within the county, but they aren't updated very often. Norfolk is a bit more of a mystery as dozens of companies operate bus services in the county and each is responsible for its own leaflets or flyers. You can pick up a number at places like Norwich Bus Station, but I must admit, I am still discovering routes in Norfolk I didn't know existed.

In addition, Essex and Suffolk produce helpful maps (free) showing bus routes throughout those counties.

Increasingly, I plan my bus journeys with the help of www.traveline.info which generally has the most up to date information regarding timetables and routes (but even that is not always perfect, as I have discovered). You can also print yourself off maps that show you where the buses stop. This can be particularly helpful if you are travelling to a less familiar place. Not everywhere has a bus station. I needed such a map when I visited Bishops Stortford, for instance.

If you are relying on making a tight connection or the last bus out of a place, it is helpful to have a 'plan B'. One or two of the trips described here required such a change of itinerary, as you will see. The odd train or taxi might be a necessary part of getting home the same day.

Increasingly, our buses are becoming more accessible to those less mobile. A number of routes now guarantee a wheelchair-friendly bus. Sometimes I have travelled with people who are a little less able than myself. I am pleased to say problems have been few.

At the time of going to print in October 2010, all information in this book was accurate, and all expeditions had been tried at least once. The author cannot be responsible for changes in routes and timetables that might come about after that. As has been discovered, not all timetabling changes are for the worse.

This book makes little reference to using a bus-pass on Ipswich, Norwich & Cambridge park-and-ride services, though this is an important function of the card and not to be forgotten.

Expedition 1: From Bungay to North Walsham and back

Bus 580: Bungay to Beccles: 25 minutes
Bus 581: Beccles to Gt. Yarmouth: 43 minutes
Bus SA6: Gt. Yarmouth to North Walsham: 1 hour 17 minutes
Bus 55: North Walsham to Norwich: 43 minutes
(Also services 5C and 210 operate this journey)
Bus 588: Norwich to Bungay: 46 minutes

This journey could have started and finished anywhere along the Waveney valley - Diss or Harleston for example. Readers of my earlier book will have read about journeys along the route covered by the 580. This is a superb journey, running by way of Geldeston to Beccles. The route has now been divided into two, but in reality it is one long lovely journey that continues on across the Haddiscoe marshes and past Fritton to Great Yarmouth. There are so many places you could stop and while away a few hours. Buses ply this route about hourly in each direction.

> **Alternatives:** You could leave the bus at Geldeston and walk to the Geldeston Locks Inn. Unsure of your way? There is even a map on a building opposite the bus stop at Geldeston. At St. Olaves, there is the old priory and the Bell Inn beside the river to enjoy. A little further on, Fritton Lake or the Redwings horse sanctuary are beside the route.

If you are following my expedition, stay on the bus as far as the Market Gates at Yarmouth. It's not the prettiest place in the world, but you can find out where to catch your next bus before exploring Yarmouth a little. You'll find there is a strange juxta-positioning of the ancient with the new, as this picture shows.

Medieval walls are sandwiched between modern car-parks and shopping centres. The old Fisherman's Hospital and the magnificent parish church lie just off the market-place. And the dockland areas offer all kinds of delights including the almost obligatory boat-trips.

The journey to North Walsham from Yarmouth takes you through parts of the Norfolk Broads. After leaving Caister, you cross Ormesby and Rollesby Broads before making for Potter Heigham. The bus route follows the old road and you cross the River Thurne by way of a very hump-backed bridge.

> **Alternatives:** There are boat-trips to be had here. Or walk along the river to the east as far as Martham or Somerton (use Ordnance Survey Explorer map OL40) and return to Yarmouth on the 1 or 1A. If you stay on the North Walsham bus as far as Catfield or Sutton, you can walk the mile or so to Hickling, one of the loveliest of the broads (The Pleasure Boat Inn beside the broad is a good place to make for).

The bus continues to Stalham and over Wayford Bridge before heading north to Walsham. You could stop at Bengate and follow the Weaver's Way back to Stalham where, on its return, this bus will take you to Yarmouth, or you might catch the 12 or 12A to Norwich (they run almost hourly 6 days a week).

North Walsham is a small but interesting town. Check out the church with its ruined tower, the cat pottery or the motorcycle museum. Buses run from here frequently in most directions. You could visit Holt, Cromer, Sheringham or, Monday to Friday, try service 34 which returns you to Stalham By-Pass (very close to the town) by way of Bacton Priory, Mundesley and Happisburgh.

On this occasion, I chose to make my way to Norwich using service 55, which takes a quite quick and direct route via Coltishall (Visited on another occasion - see Expedition 36) into the centre of Norwich. You find a lot of Norwich-bound buses do not use the bus-station. A number of stops are spread along streets nearby. You soon get used to this. The timetables name the streets and some have maps to help you. The bus I needed next, for example, left from St Stephen's Street, only a stone's throw from the bus-station. I'd used the 588 route before. It is a pleasant run through Trowse, Poringland

and a number of villages before taking a circular route around Bungay. I arrived back in plenty of time for a cup of coffee in the small restaurant beside Bungay Castle.

Bungay

Expedition 2: From Brandon to King's Lynn, then around the North Norfolk coast before returning home to Stowmarket by bus and train

Bus 28: Brandon to King's Lynn: 1 hour 10 minutes
         (or Bus 40 from Thetford: 1 hour 6 minutes)
Coast hopper bus: King's Lynn to Sheringham: 2 hr. 17 min.
Bus 44: Sheringham to Norwich: 1 hour 19 min.
By train: Norwich to Stowmarket: 29 minutes

      In my previous bus-pass book, I described the route from Brandon to King's Lynn. When a county bus-pass meant you had to begin or end a journey in your own county, this was one of the longest routes transporting you out of Suffolk. King's Lynn, as I showed, has much to recommend it, but on this occasion, I was intent on travelling

9

further. Instead of Brandon, you might use Thetford as your starting point, catching a service 40 bus.

From King's Lynn, you can catch the Coasthopper bus. This is designed to attract tourists and does exactly what it says on the side. The delights of the North Norfolk seaside towns and villages can be sampled in a measure of comfort as you take a leisurely two-hour excursion. You'll probably want to do this more than once, as there are places along the way that warrant further examination.

Castle Rising is a lovely old village with a fine castle to visit. Remember, these buses now run about every hour in both directions, though some begin and end at Hunstanton. Hunstanton is a place best seen out of season, unless you fancy braving the North Sea. Another place that is also worth a few hours of your time is Burnham Market, which more than reminds you of its Nelson connections. You get splendid views of coast and marsh as you travel around Wells, Stiffkey, Morston and Blakeney and there are endless coastal-path walks to be enjoyed (refer to OS Explorer maps 251 & 252).

Alternative: If you get off the bus at Wells, you can catch a service 29 to Fakenham. This takes you via the ancient pilgrimage centre of Walsingham, which is well worth a visit in its own right. At Fakenham, the X29 will convey you the rest of the way to Norwich.

I stayed on the Coasthopper and was glad I did. The areas around Holkham and Cley are a must for the naturalist (don't forget your binoculars). Even from the bus, you have every chance of seeing marsh harriers, several varieties of goose and wading birds aplenty. This is a truly wonderful bus ride.

Once at Sheringham, you have plenty of choices. Enjoy Sheringham or move on to Cromer. Alternatively, buses or steam trains will take you to Holt (Holt Station is well out of the town and you will probably require a further means of transport to reach the town-centre).

Sheringham Station

Holt

After just an hour or so in Sheringham, I caught a 44 which went to Norwich by way of Cromer and the lovely market town of Aylsham (about which more is written later - see expedition 4)

Given the choice of another two buses and over two hours to return me to Stowmarket, I instead opted for a twenty-nine minute train journey that cost me just under ten pounds. The day which had started bright was now wet and slightly bleak. This proved a comfortable and civilised way to finish my day.

Expedition 3: From Stowmarket to Colchester via Hadleigh and back via Ipswich

Bus 462: Stowmarket to Hadleigh: 42 minutes
Bus 755: Hadleigh to Colchester: 57 minutes
Bus 93: Colchester to Ipswich: 1 hour 15 min.
Bus 88: Ipswich to Stowmarket: 42 minutes

From Stowmarket, there are a number of options regarding how one might reach Colchester. I chose the route I did, as, at the time, I would be getting straight off one bus in Hadleigh and onto another bound for Colchester. Failing that I'd have had to have waited for the next bus or moved on to Sudbury and then to Colchester, delaying my arrival by over an hour. This time I was lucky.

I could, of course, have gone the way I finally returned, or travelled to Bury or Sudbury (753) to catch my bus to Colchester.

The Stowmarket to Hadleigh route is rural in the extreme. You circle Wattisham Base before moving across county through Naughton and Whatfield. The 755 from Hadleigh to Colchester travels through the attractive villages of Polstead, Stoke-by-Nayland and Higham.

Alternative: Some later buses on the 755 route pass through East Bergholt. Using OS Explorer map 196, you can leave the bus there, and walk the magnificent couple of miles down to the river at Flatford and along in a westerly direction to Dedham. The walk is spectacular, Dedham village is a delight and, if you have time, you can even hire a boat for a while. Routes 247 and 87A run from Dedham to Colchester.

Colchester Castle

Colchester bus-station, like much of central Colchester is, at the time of writing, undergoing something of a remodelling. However, it is close to shops, Castle and other attractions such as the Natural History Museum (in an old church). There is a great deal to see and do in Colchester - the Tourist Information Centre is just around the corner from the bus-station, opposite the entrance to Castle Park.

Coming back to Ipswich the 93 route runs through parts of East Bergholt, Capel St. Mary and Washbrook. I was lucky again to step off one bus and onto another (88), to allow me wing my way back to Stowmarket.

Expedition 4: From Diss to Wroxham and back via Aylsham

Bus SIM1: Diss to Norwich: 1 hour 8 min.
Bus 123 or 12A: Norwich to Wroxham: 38 - 40 minutes
Bure Valley Railway: Wroxham to Aylsham: 45 minutes
Bus 44: Aylsham to Norwich: 42 minutes
Bus SIM2: Norwich to Diss: 44 minutes

You could begin this journey in a number of places such as Bungay, Harleston, the Pulhams, or by using any one of the once-a-week buses to Norwich (Saturday - Route 25 - from Brandon; Thursday - route 563 - from Aldeburgh; Monday - route 564 - from Wickham Market), though you will have to work out appropriate return routes in each case.

Diss Bus Station, as with the other start-points quoted, is close to a car park, should you need to drive in to begin your excursion. The bus route remains close to the A140, stopping at Scole, Dickleburgh, Long Stratton and other Norfolk villages before offering

Close to Norwich bus-station

a choice of stops in Norwich. For this trip, get off at St. Stephens Street and walk around the corner to Norwich bus-station. With luck, you'll have plenty of time to catch a 123 to Wroxham. You may even have time to have a coffee at the bus-station and arm your-self with further timetables.

A warning - planning bus trips in Norfolk is harder than in Suffolk or Essex. Separate bus companies produce their own literature, so you don't have the advantage of booklets that combine all the available routes in one area. Sometimes you find yourself consulting a bundle of fliers, booklets and sheets of paper just to see which companies offer which routes and when.

The 123 and 12A are not the only routes that will take you to Wroxham. A little more direct is the Neaves Buses route 36, but it runs less frequently. It is easy when passing through Broadland along main roads to see very little of the beauty of it, so a number of serious alternatives are included here. The route to Wroxham is not particularly spectacular. Salhouse village is well away from the Broad that bears that name, though you could get off there and walk the mile or so down to the water. Wroxham and its other-side-of-the-river partner, Hoveton are not the most attractive of places at first glance, though you can walk beside the river and hire boats there. Boat-trips are recommended, though I'd suggest staying on the bus as far as Horning and taking a trip from there.

> **Alternatives:** Horning, Ludham Bridge and the village of Ludham are all places where you can get close to river and broads. Boat and cycle hire are vailable in a number of places. If you are a keen walker, leave the bus just beyond Ludham Bridge and, using OS Explorer map OL40, walk lanes and footpaths to St. Benet's Abbey ruins, beloved of Norwich-School artists. Remember, buses run this route hourly in both directions between Norwich and Stalham.

Wroxham Broad

For a large part of the year, the Bure Valley Railway runs trains between Wroxham and Aylsham(www.bvrw.co.uk).

Though these may or may not link easily with your bus, the trip can be well worth the wait. Most trains are steam-powered, and the countryside you pass through is wonderful. You can either take a one-way journey and return, as I did from Aylsham by bus, or enjoy the full eighteen mile round-trip and come back on the 123 to Norwich. Either way, it makes the day a bit special. The restaurant at Aylsham Station serves meals as well as light refreshments.

A number of services will take you from Aylsham to Norwich. The 44 goes hourly from Cromer and passes through Aylsham Market Place. I used the hourly service (50) from Sheringham to Norwich, which took slightly longer, but still returned me to Norwich in plenty of time to catch my bus back to Diss.

Expedition 5: From Bury to Cambridge, Haverhill & Sudbury

Bus 11: Bury to Newmarket: 30 minutes
Bus 10: Newmarket to Cambridge: 1 hour 16 minutes
Bus 13: Cambridge to Haverhill: 1 hour 5 minutes
Bus 236: Haverhill to Sudbury: 50 minutes
Bus 753: Sudbury to Bury: 60 minutes

I had an appointment in Cambridge, but was in no great hurry, so I took a fairly circuitous route getting there. The journey to Newmarket is straightforward enough. From there, it is possible to continue to Cambridge along a fast route I'd used a number of times before. This time it would be different. The service 10 wanders through a host of villages before deciding there can be no more to visit and finally making for Cambridge. It takes a long while leaving Newmarket for a start. (You know you're still in Newmarket, as all the roads are named after horses, trainers or jockeys.) The villages along the route are worthy of attention. Burwell has a small museum and a number of very old buildings.

> **Alternative:** As you head for Swaffham Prior, you pass the car park for walks along the Devil's Dyke. If you get off here, you can work a pleasant walk, returning to the same place and catching one of the buses that appear hourly in both directions.

As you enter Swaffham Prior, you spot the windmill beside the water-tower. The village has two very similar churches. One has been retired and is now a gallery. The other has a magnificent set of stained glass windows by way of a war memorial. The closer, you get to Cambridge, the more aware you become of the white chalky soil. Passing through Lode, you come close to Anglesey Abbey (National Trust), which is well worth a visit.

Cambridge has so much to offer, I'd recommend several days exploring. It is the land of the bicycle, as this picture shows.

On this occasion, however, I had a circuit to complete, so after an early lunch, I was on my way to Haverhill. The route was a less familiar one to me, but interesting. You pass close to Linton Zoo and enjoy views of some lovely countryside before an almost interminable crawl around the housing estates of Haverhill.

I had just a short stop before my 236 bus to Sudbury. I've noticed before what a superb journey this is. Like a lot of routes, you see it in an entirely different way coming in the opposite direction. We passed through Clare, Cavendish and Long Melford before entering Sudbury. It was, however, at that time in the afternoon when schools were emptying their classrooms into all passing transport, and it was a far from peaceful journey. Still, the final leg of my day's excursion was lovely. From Sudbury to Bury passes through Lavenham and a number of other pretty villages, before making for Bury St. Edmunds. This trip is strongly recommended.

Expedition 6: From Bildeston to Maldon and circling back via Tollesbury

Bus 112: Bildeston to Sudbury: 28 minutes
Bus 753: Sudbury to Colchester: 49 minutes
Bus 75: Colchester to Maldon: 56 minutes
Bus 95: Maldon to Tollesbury: 28 minutes
Bus 92: Tollesbury to Colchester: 40 minutes
Bus 753: Colchester to Sudbury: 50 minutes
Bus 112: Sudbury to Bildeston: 34 minutes

I began this trip earlier than any before, leaving Bildeston at 7.18 in the morning. This may soon mean paying for your first journey of the day (see page 5). In my previous book (Exploring Suffolk by Bus-Pass) I pointed out what a good place Bildeston is for beginning and ending a journey. You can park in the square (free) and a variety of buses come and go, distributing passengers to Ipswich (service 111), Sudbury (112), Stowmarket (461) and Bury (376).

The route from Bildeston to Sudbury passes through some of the most attractive of Suffolk villages including Chelsworth and

Monks Eleigh. Similarly, the 753 route out of Sudbury, passes through Bures and Wormingford. The road hugs the River Stour before making for Colchester. I stayed aboard as far as the bus-station. Most passengers had already disembarked in the town.

Buses run between Maldon and Colchester hourly throughout the day and evening. You approach Maldon, crossing the river before rising steeply into the town. It is worth noting that if you have any doubts as to where to catch a bus in Maldon, the Tesco's stop just below the town is on most routes.

Maldon Quay

The town itself has much to offer. The Hythe Quay, with its old Thames barges, is my favourite place. Dependent on the tides, sailing trips are available. Around the town are dotted other places of interest including the Museum in the park, the Moot Hall and the Plume Library. Heritage trail leaflets are available from the Tourist Information Centre. Northey Island (National Trust) can be visited by appointment but the causeway to it is only uncovered at low tide.

I stayed only an hour in Maldon (not really long enough) before boarding a bus for Tollesbury. This takes you along the flatlands (rarely more than ten metres above sea-level) of Goldhanger and Tolleshunt, before wending as far East as the bus goes, to the Square at Tollesbury.

> **Alternative:** Why not stop at Goldhanger, where the footpaths will lead you (using OS Explorer map 176) to the creeks and saltings beside the Blackwater, giving you views of Osea Island, which is reached by a causeway that is only above tide-level for a few hours a day.

Having left the bus in the Square at Tollesbury, surrounded by churchyards and the occasional pub, you can choose to follow the heritage trail around the village. I walked directly down to the waterfront where a cluster of buildings house small industries, mostly relating to boating. This is another place very much at the mercy of the sea. As you look across miles of marshes and creeks, you glimpse Mersea Island to the East.

On walking back to the Square, I boarded a service 92 bus for Colchester. This is one of the most attractive routes I have taken in Essex. Skirting Salcott and Wigborough, the bus made for Layer de-la-Haye, crossing Abberton Reservoir by way of one of two bridges in that area. We also passed the Visitor Centre.

> **Alternative:** If you get off the bus beside the bridge, you can enjoy views across the reservoir with its fabulous array of wildfowl. The Visitor Centre, less than half a mile further on is open from Tuesday to Sunday throughout the year and offers refreshments. From there, if you leave time, you can follow footpaths through Layer Breton to the magnificent Tudor gatehouse, Layer Marney Tower. This is open from Sunday to Thursday during Spring and Summer. From there it is only under a mile's walk to the Colchester-Tiptree Road where bus route 95 passes hourly.

Returning to Colchester, I found my next two buses linked perfectly and for all the miles I'd travelled and all the places I'd seen, I was back in Bildeston well before 5:30 p.m.

Expedition 6A: From Maldon to Burnham-on-Crouch & Bradwell

Bus 31X: Maldon to Burnham: 38 minutes
Bus D4: Burnham to Bradwell: 39 minutes
Bus D1: Bradwell to Maldon: 49 minutes

Having reached Maldon, you can easily enjoy an afternoon exploring this corner of Essex. Catch the bus outside All Saints Church in the centre of the town. The 31X takes you into a world of stables and rookeries, as far removed from the public conception of Essex as it is possible to find. This short trip through Mundon and Latchingdon works its way towards Burnham, which is a real delight. There are antique and gift shops to suit all tastes and tea rooms boasting 'home-made cakes on vintage china.' In the summer, you can take boat trips or the ferry over the water to Wallasea Island.

The clock tower at Burnham-on-Crouch

Alternative: The other side of the ferry, you can enjoy walking around the nature reserve (use O.S. Explorer map 176) Then walk to Canewdon or Ballards Gore and use Bus 60 to Southend, Bus 3 to Chelmsford & Bus 31 to Maldon or Bus 70 to Colchester. These buses run fairly late and enable trips to be organised well into the evening.

My second bus of this expedition was the D4, which, like most buses in Burnham is caught from near the clock tower. The route began with bendy lanes and high hedges. Again we visited Southminster with its ancient and precarious-looking church tower, before wending our way across flatlands to Tillingham and Bradwell.

You need either a lot of time to explore Bradwell or very little. Firstly, it is quite spread out. The D4 bus takes you as far as the marina, which is a good mile beyond the village. If, as I did, you discover you've made a mistake by staying on the bus longer than intended, just come back a stop or two and get off near the church. Walking up the road past the school, you'll encounter a pub, at which point it will be at least another mile before you reach the sea and the Saxon Chapel of St. Peter on the Wall. This is a wonderfully bleak and deserted corner of Essex.

The D1 bus begins its journey back to Maldon from a cluster of houses along the East End Road. This is a pleasant and ambling journey along the Blackwater estuary and at one point very nearly brings you to the river's edge at St. Lawrence Bay.

The mounting post outside Bradwell church

Alternative: St. Lawrence Bay is well worth a visit all of its own. The bus turns round just before the riverside. If you have plenty of time, leave it here and walk up river as far as Steeple or Mayland, both of which are on this bus-route.

Just five hours after beginning my journey, I was stepping off the bus in Maldon at exactly the same point at which my expedition had begun.

Expedition 7: Bury St. Edmunds to Cambridge and back, suggesting alternative ways to return

Bus 11: Bury to Cambridge via Newmarket: 1 hour 7 minutes
Bus 16: Cambridge to Haverhill: 50 minutes
Bus 344/345: Haverhill to Bury: 62/52 minutes

The journey from Bury to Cambridge is probably the fastest and most direct of any in East Anglia. From Bury, the route follows the A14 before veering off through Kentford on its way across the heath into Newmarket. The stop is brief and designed to link with the Ely bus (12). After that, the bus uses the old A45 route to Cambridge and travels at some speed before branching off and following bus-lanes into Cambridge. You pass the airport, the football ground and a medieval leper hospital, so there is a fair bit to look out for. The bus-station is right amidst the colleges and you find you are in the centre of Cambridge immediately. Remember (as will be shown from later expeditions) you can travel a long way from Cambridge with your bus-pass in a variety of directions.

I'm not a great lover of big towns, but Cambridge is definitely different. Shopaholics could run amok here. Lovers of architecture and history could spend a lifetime discovering this place. I love all the old bookshops, and the plethora of museums. It seems round every corner there is something to catch your eye. Street entertainers abound and there are so many exhibitions and places to appeal to your sense of curiosity. Try (afternoons only) the house at Kettle's Yard.

Out of season, most of the punts lie idle and on a fine autumn day... why not? The Fitzwilliam Museum has one of the finest collections outside London, and if you have the time, cast an eye over the advertising posters tied to every available railing and see what

else takes your fancy. Cambridge has so much to offer, I was only too glad to know I'd be revisiting it a number of times during the writing of this book. And if you want to acquaint yourself with the city, a free bus (free for everybody) circles the centre, enabling you to identify the main landmarks.

As regards my return to Bury, I chose to head for Haverhill, taking an entirely diffferent route from that in expedition 5, in the knowledge that the journey from there to Bury via Kedington and Chedburgh would be a delight on a bright autumn day. Two slightly different routes alternate here; both are intensely rural, and a pleasant way of seeing Suffolk at its best.

Alternatives: I could easily have returned the way I had come. That would have been quick and efficient. However, I could have chosen to break my journey at Newmarket, returning to Bury on the 312 which ambles along a picturesque route, taking a further hour or so. From Newmarket, I could equally easily have caught the 400 or 401 to Mildenhall (about 40 minutes), returning to Bury on the 355 or 356 (both about 35 minutes and following equally attractive routes)

Expedition 8: Mildenhall to Huntingdon and St. Ives

Bus 356: Mildenhall to Bury: 37 minutes
Bus 11: Bury to Cambridge: 1 hour 7 minutes
Bus 1A or 1B: Cambridge to Huntingdon: 58/56 minutes
Bus 5: Huntingdon to St. Ives: 25 minutes
Bus CITI5: St. Ives to Cambridge: 1 hour 19 minutes
Bus 12: Cambridge to Newmarket: 35 minutes
Bus 400/401: Newmarket to Mildenhall: 30/39 minutes

      This was a bit of a trek across Cambridgeshire to see what bus travel was like in that part of the country. I began from Mildenhall taking a route I'd enjoyed before, reaching Bury in plenty of time to head for Cambridge. A number of routes run to St. Ives and Huntingdon, meaning that those places are linked in such a way you can travel between them several times an hour until quite late in the evening.

      Service 5 heads up the A14; then on crossing the river Great Ouse just before St. Ives, you catch that splendid view of the bridge that makes St. Ives one of the most attractive fenland towns. Close to the bus-station is the auction room, which holds Saturday auctions once a fortnight. The riverside area is lovely, especially on a fine day. I suggest you explore the old town quay and the chapel on the bridge. The town also boasts a number of other fine old buildings.

The bridge at St. Ives

You may choose to travel directly to Huntingdon. The 1A route takes you through the village of Houghton with its water mill (National Trust). Houghton is a lovely village with riverside walks. Remember plenty of buses ply this route and the nearby relief road. Service 1B instead travels to the main gate of RAF Wyton with its fine old Canberra standing guard in front of the base.

You enter Huntingdon along the river. In summer time there are boats for hire. The old parts of Huntingdon are well worth exploring. There is the Cromwell museum, just one of countless reminders of the town's most famous old boy.

Huntingdon

I returned to St. Ives using one of the the quickest routes (service 5), but chose to finish the journey to Cambridge by the ambling service CITI5. It was a double-decker and gave me great views across the fenlands around Fenstanton, Over and Willingham. At the time of writing, a guided busway was being constructed that will run soon across Cambridge and out as far as St. Ives. The construction work diverted us, but offered us some good views of the work that is underway.

My way back to Mildenhall via Newmarket was efficient but unremarkable. Once again it became clear just how far you can travel in a day with a bus-pass.

Expedition 9: Halesworth - Norwich - Lowestoft - Halesworth on a Sunday

Bus 588: Halesworth to Norwich: 1 hour 5 minutes
Bus X2: Norwich to Lowestoft: 1 hour 14 minutes
               (or X1 via Acle & Yarmouth)
Bus 601: Lowestoft to Halesworth: 1 hour 24 minutes

This trip works either way round, seven days a week. Sunday buses are less plentiful than on other days of the week, but this circuit and its variations are easy to use, as at least 5 buses run all the routes followed.

The Norwich service from Halesworth and Bungay was well used. By the time we reached Norwich, the bus was quite full. We moved rapidly to Bungay, then on through the villages of Ditchingham, Hedingham and Brooke on a bleak, wet day. However, in late October, Christmas shoppers were very much in evidence and the town was comfortably busy.

When I was ready to move on, I had a choice between the X2 and the X1. The X1 takes you to Acle and Yarmouth before plunging south to Gorleston and Lowestoft. This is the less attractive route, though the marshlands after Acle are interesting. Here, flat water-meadows are carved up by dikes, and old wind-pumps fill the skyline. Swans, egrets and Egyptian geese can be seen. Otherwise, the journey is unremarkable. But this service has the convenience of operating a half-hour apart from the X2.

The journey on the X2, via Loddon and Beccles is more rural and, I believe, more enjoyable. As with a number of Sunday routes, it takes a slightly different route from the rest of the week. As well as passing through Loddon and Beccles, we saw a number of villages along the Waverney Valley before entering Carlton Colville. Then you find, the journey becomes a succession of roundabouts - I think Lowestoft is trying to rival Milton Keynes for roundabouts. I did not intend to remain in Lowestoft on such a wet wintry day. But on finer days, other possibilities offer themselves up on the next section of my journey.

> **Alternative:** When you finally escape the environs of Lowestoft, you find yourself heading for Wrentham. Here, the reasonably fit walker might plan a walk around Benacre or Covehithe using OS Explorer map 231.

Only on a Sunday will you find the 601 bus route runs via Southwold as far as Halesworth. Once you have left Lowestoft and Kessingland, the journey is an attractive one, approaching Southwold by way of Wrentham, Wangford and Reydon. It runs rather later than the 601 does during the week, so there is plenty of opportunity to spend time in Southwold.

> **Alternative:** Why not use an O.S. Explorer map 231 to find your way along the coast path to the passenger ferry. If it is operating, you could cross the Blythe there to Walberswick. Otherwise, walk upstream to the old railway bridge and follow tracks across Walberswick Common and Nature Reserve to Blythburgh. It is about a four-mile walk, one of the most beautiful in East Anglia and amazing for its wildlife. On reaching Blythburgh, you are back on the bus route.

The Blyth estuary near Blythburgh

The final section of the journey runs through Wenhaston, Blyford and Holton. For the first time that day, the sun came out and the Blyth valley looked awesome in Autumn.

Expedition 10: The edge of the Breckland by bus and fold-up bike

Bus 338: Bury St. Edmunds to Hopton: 60 minutes
Bike to Euston via Knettishall Heath
Bus 332: Euston to Culford: 33 minutes
Bike to Flempton via West Stow
Bus 355: Flempton to Bury St. Edmunds: 15 minutes

What we need is an integrated transport system. If you have a fold-up bike, you've got one. I tried this out for the first time when writing *'Exploring Suffolk by bus-pass.'* The route across Knettishall Heath appeared in that book as an alternative suggestion. This time I tried it for real.

Technically, bus drivers can make a small charge for bikes (and dogs, and large parcels), but rarely do. By the time I reached Hopton, I was the last person on the bus. I put my bike together and started out. It was a cold bright crisp autumn morning and the countryside looked just great! The route stays just in Suffolk and follows a road that on this occasion seemed devoid of traffic. It is worth mentioning that Knettishall Heath has a toilet. It is a wonderful place to picnic in summertime. I found wildlife there in plenty - deer (roe & muntjak), squirrels and a host of hedgerow birds on the berries.

> **Alternative:** I began from Hopton, but fold-up bikes only have little wheels and don't travel very fast. Ideally, and to make this less of a rush, you might leave the bus at the junction just after Coney Weston Hall, heading for Knettishall Heath from there. It cuts the cycle ride by a mile or so.

My first cycle ride was a distance of about six miles. The route is fairly flat and undemanding. At Euston, you need to cycle past one entrance to Euston Hall (open from June to September on Thursdays and a number of Sundays) and wait for the 332 bus by the triangle at the north of the village (use OS Explorer map 229). I had already identified this bus-route as being one of the most attractive in East Anglia. Then, just before Culford, (still on the same map) I left the bus at Brockley Corner and cycled the short distance to West

Stow and on to Flempton, where there was time for a brief refresher in the Greyhound before boarding a bus for Bury beside the church.

The lake at West Stow

Alternative: Strongly recommended is turning right in West Stow and heading for the Saxon Village. As well as the reconstructed houses you can enjoy wonderful nature walks beside the River Lark, and a splendid tea-room with views of the best bird-feeders you'll find anywhere. Afterwards, you can flag down your bus (service 355) where the road meets the B1112 between Icklingham and Lackford.

The 355 bus runs two-hourly between Mildenhall and Bury. It is only a short trip back to the bus station. On the day in question, I'd been given a lift into Bury and needed to return to Stowmarket. I guess I was not the most popular person in the world, boarding an already crowded bus on Market day with a fold-up bike, but it worked and I arrived back with just a short pedal home to complete a very satisfactory day.

Kings Lynn (left) and Cromer (right), opposite ends of the North Norfolk coast, linked by the Coasthopper bus which passes through Blakeney and Cley and many other lovely parts of that stretch of coastline.

The historic town of Dunmow in Essex, reached from Chelmsford by service 42A

Oundle near Peterborough lies on route
X4 - see expedition 40 in this book

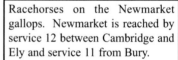

Racehorses on the Newmarket
gallops. Newmarket is reached by
service 12 between Cambridge and
Ely and service 11 from Bury.

Expedition 11: From Bury to Oxford and back

Bus 11: Bury to Cambridge: 1 hour 12 minutes
Bus X5: Cambridge to Oxford: 3 hours 15 minutes
The same in reverse coming home.

I know, Oxford isn't in East Anglia and, even allowing for global warming altering the coastline, it probably never will be. But I was interested to see just how far away from the region you could get in a day using only regular service buses.

I started early from Bury, having parked my car for the day behind the bus-station (it cost me £2.70). Normally, it's a quick and easy journey to Cambridge via Newmarket, but as we were travelling at rush-hour, we took rather longer than the scheduled time to make our way into the city centre. There are bus-lanes, but reaching them was the problem. Therefore, I didn't catch my intended bus to Oxford. However, the X5 runs every half-hour throughout a long day, so I wasn't waiting long. Fortunately, with readjusted timetables, buses from Bury now miss the worst of the traffic.

Your bus pass clocks in at 9:30 a.m. In Suffolk, this wasn't an issue and I rode for free to Cambridge. However, as Cambridgeshire do enforce this limit, I had to pay for the first half-hour of my journey - to St. Neots (It cost £2.50). After that, I travelled free. The coaches used on this route are comfortable and high-spec. Though I was to spend a long time on buses, at least, I could enjoy the journey.

The route out of Cambridge passes the American cemetery at Madingley and the Cambridge University observatory. Beyond that, it doesn't take very long before you find yourself approaching St. Neots. We passed through the market place and over the river beside the park and out towards Bedford.

The coach stops in Bedford for at least ten minutes. There is time to find toilets at the bus-station and to buy newspapers and nibbles. Then it was on to Milton Keynes. This is a town that gets a bit of a bad press, but I must admit I rather like it. The centre is most impressive with its long boulevards and massive stores and malls. It is one of the few places I know that positively welcomes motorised traffic and had I not been bound for Oxford, I'd have gladly spent a few hours there.

The bus moved on, stopping at the edge of Buckingham to take on passengers. This is another place worth visiting, but as this route only runs along the outskirts, you would need to catch a local bus to the town centre.

From there, we travelled to Bicester, before making for Oxford. If Cambridge is bicycle-city, then Oxford is bus-city. Bus lanes prevail, buses and coaches stream in and out and around the city in all

directions. This is, after all, the centre of England.

My plan was, as always, to return the same day, which left me a maximum of two and a half hours if I was to catch the last bus back to Bury (though buses as far as Newmarket run rather later) This meant a brief glimpse at a place that warrants much further inspection. Still, eating lunch beside the gleaming spires and a short wander around the colleges was great fun.

The return journey was enlivened by a driver who got a bit of a move-on between stops so he'd have time for a fag every so often whilst he waited for the timetable to catch him up. Another thing of note is the red kites that are becoming plentiful in parts of Oxfordshire. Not for the first time travelling this way, I saw one.

The final part of the journey back was in the dark, and it is true, the day had been a bit of a trek, but this route opens up all kinds of possibilities - Shopping at Milton Keynes would give you three or four hours before you needed to return. Exploring Buckingham would give you at least three hours there. And if you wanted longer in

Oxford, then you could start and finish your day at Newmarket.

My bus journeys have all been day trips. For those more adventurous, having reached Oxford by the middle of the day, you can find further routes, particularly to the south and west. From Bury in a day, you could reach Gloucester or Southampton using only regular service routes (with your bus-pass).

Expedition 12: From Bury, across the fens and back

Bus 11: Bury to Cambridge: 1 hour 5 minutes
Bus X9: Cambridge to March: 1 hour 51 minutes
Bus 56: March to Wisbech: 39 minutes
Bus X1: Wisbech to Kings Lynn: 28 minutes
Bus 37: Kings Lynn to Downham Market: 37 minutes
Bus 40: Downham Market to Thetford: 74 minutes (schooldays)
Bus 332: Thetford to Bury: 51 minutes

This was the planned route, but things don't always work out as planned. The second half of my day took on a different shape, as I shall explain.

Having reached Cambridge, it was only a short wait before the hourly X9 bus appeared. When I first tried this route, the X9 went all the way to Wisbech. Now you need to change buses in March.

You are slow leaving Cambridge by this route, but having left the Science Parks behind, the open spaces of the fens open up. From the top of a double-decker, you get a great view. The countryside is flat, but far from featureless. We turned through Stretham, passing both church and windmill (now a house). As we left the village and rejoined the main road, Ely Cathedral came into view in all its magnificence - it really is out of proportion to the small town it serves.

In my earlier book, I have written about the delights of Ely. I could easily have stayed longer there, but opted to continue my journey. I had a long way to go.

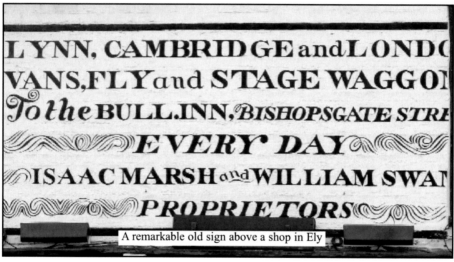

LYNN, CAMBRIDGE and LONDO
VANS, FLY and STAGE WAGGON
To the BULL.INN, BISHOPSGATE STRI
EVERY DAY
ISAAC MARSH and WILLIAM SWAI
PROPRIETORS

A remarkable old sign above a shop in Ely

The Fenland across the Isle of Ely has much to grab your interest. The little village of Sutton in the Isle has a very fine church (open daily). The fields were waterlogged and lakes and dykes were full. The landscape was dotted with wintering gulls and golden plover.

After a brief wait in March for the 56 bus, it was on towards Wisbech. There was an array of wind generators and at one point we followed a rusty rail track that clearly hadn't seen service for some time. You could sense a real feeling of isolation.

Eventually, we heaved into Wisbech bus-station, an unpleas-
ant and uncared-for area. The town is a strange mix. It has its
riverfront where grand old merchants' houses sit beside the Nene.
There is the old Port area, now a place of regeneration. The town too
has interesting corners, though it lacks the charm of old King's Lynn.

Wisbech

The X1 bus runs every half-hour between Peterborough and
Lowestoft. I had travelled along parts of its long route before. On
this occasion, I only expected to use this bus briefly, but as I
mentioned earlier, the best laid plans of mice and men...

We arrived at King's Lynn more than 15 minutes late. I just
missed my connection. I could see the Downham Market bus leaving
as we pulled in. This meant I had to revise my plans. The rearranged
journey continued as follows...

Bus X1: Kings Lynn to Norwich: 1 hour 51 minutes
Train: Norwich to Diss: 16 minutes
Bus 304: Diss to Bury: 1 hour 29 minutes

From Lynn to Norwich was a route I'd followed before,
through Swaffham and Dereham. In Norwich, I hopped on a bus

down to the railway station. The train journey (costing £7.80) enabled me to catch the last bus back to Bury, an ambling tour taking me through most of the villages of north-west Suffolk. This was also in the dark, which was a pity as it is an attractive route during the daylight hours. This ended up being an exhausting day with too long spent on buses. With better luck, it would have been more relaxing and more interesting. Still, you can't win them all!

Excursion 13: From Hadleigh to Brightlingsea, with a good walk thrown in.

Bus 755: Hadleigh to Colchester: 55 minutes
Walk to Essex University at Wivenhoe
Bus 61: Essex University to Wivenhoe Co-op: 6 minutes
Bus 78X: Wivenhoe to Brightlingsea: 26 minutes
Bus 78X: Brightlingsea to Colchester: 43 minutes
Bus 755: Colchester to Hadleigh: 1 hour 5 minutes
    (or from Norman Way on schooldays, Bus 971: 75 minutes)

I actually began my trip from Stowmarket. The 462 then ran an early morning bus to Hadleigh. You could be cutting it a bit fine if linking with the Colchester bus from Hadleigh, but although we started ten minutes late, the driver managed to make up all the time and I caught the 755 to Colchester. The Stowmarket - Hadleigh route has now become more complicated.

The 755 follows a route I'd enjoyed before. You pass through attractive villages such as East Bergholt and Stratford St. Mary.

I had it in mind to walk from the bus station to the Hythe, the old port of Colchester. I had obtained a leaflet describing the route, and began by walking down East Hill and picking up the Riverside Trail. This sounds rather more attractive than it turned out to be. Most of this part of Colchester is sad and unloved, with decaying buildings and endless graffiti. When you do have views of the River Colne, it is to play 'count the shopping trolleys.' It is a couple of miles before you see much improvement. Crossing the river and continuing past the University Quays (There is a good café there),

I began to enjoy it. Redshank, cormorant and dabchick were on show, as were several boats. One, an old barge, offers river trips.

Eventually, you reach a track to the left leading to the main university campus (after about another mile). You cross the railway (carefully) and make your way to the Boundary Road that rings the campus. Walking about a hundred yards either ahead or back will bring you to a bus stop. From there, you can catch buses (hourly) to Clacton (74) or to Brightlingsea (every half-hour). Having just seen my bus pull away, I took the first 61 that came and travelled as far as Wivenhoe Co-op. I knew from there I would be able to catch the next bus to Brightlingsea, as was the case.

The route follows the Colne Valley. My bus (78X) was a double-decker and I had excellent views.

Alternative: If you leave the bus near Alresford Station and walk over the railway and down Ford lane, you will pick up the riverside foot-paths that follow Alresford Creek towards Thorington (O.S. Explorer map 184). You can enjoy a terrific 2-3 mile walk, returning to the bus route to the south of Thorington. There are plenty of bus stops marked as the road approaches Brightlingsea.

In Brightlingsea, I left the bus close to the promenade, which looks out on Point Clear in one direction and East Mersea in another.

Though it was a cold day, it was a bright one and there was plenty to see as boats moved up and down the estuary.

> **Alternative:** I've already mentioned the delights of Mersea Island in the second edition of *'Exploring Suffolk by Bus-Pass'*. In summer, you can take the foot ferry from Brightlingsea to East Mersea, and plan a walk to link up with the West Mersea buses. (Again, use O.S. Explorer map 184)

The town of Brightlingsea is small and well laid out. It is also quite self-contained. Most of the shops you'd need are there. It has a beach and an old lido, open in the summer months. On leaving, the return journey from the centre of the town was pleasant and gave me just the right amount of time to potter in Colchester before heading back to Hadleigh.

Brightlingsea

Please note, there is an alternative bus back in the 971, but it picks up in Norman Way and it is a school bus, with all the pleasures that that may bring! Your journey home will be a good deal noisier.

Excursion 14: A pilgrimage from Diss to Walsingham and the small towns of North Norfolk

Bus S1M1: Diss to Norwich: 1 hour 8 minutes
Bus X29: Norwich to Fakenham: 1 hour 4 minutes
Bus 29: Fakenham to Walsingham: 14 minutes
Bus 29: Walsingham to Fakenham: 14 minutes
Bus 9: Fakenham to Holt: 32 minutes
Bus 4: Holt to Sheringham: 17 minutes
Bus 44: Sheringham to Norwich via Cromer: 1 hour 16 minutes
Bus S1M2: Norwich to Diss: 47 minutes (or Bus S1M1)

     Living in Stowmarket, it would have been possible to have begun and ended there, but eight buses in one day was enough for me, so I drove to Diss to begin my journey. Anyone doing the same could avoid paying for parking by driving to the top of the town and catching the service 1 bus beside the cemetery.

     This proved to be an interesting route to Norwich that involved the driver putting a forty-seater round some of the bendiest

Norwich Cathedral

41

roads in Norfolk. We passed the Burston Strike School and a number of round-towered churches such as the one at Gissing. We seemed to pick up a number of passengers in particularly remote spots. But as the sun came out, the scenery, even in winter was pleasant.

There was just long enough in Norwich to have a cup of coffee before boarding the X29 for Fakenham. Knowing I had a fairly tight connection to make, I asked the driver if this would be a problem. He assured me that on reaching Fakenham, this bus would change its route number and become the one I wanted.

It took an age to leave Norwich behind and it was at least twenty minutes before I saw farmland. Then we motored through Lenwade, and in and out of Bawdeswell, Foulsham and Guist.

> **Alternative:** Leave the bus at either Drayton or Lenwade and you will be close to Marriott's Way (see O.S. Explorer map 238). This is a lovely track, easily walkable at all times of the year, as most of it follows an old railway track. You can walk to Reepham (2-4 miles according to the route you follow) or further to Cawston or Aylsham. Eastons Coaches run an occasional service from Reepham and Cawston to Norwich. Links between Aylsham and Norwich are far more frequent.

We entered Fakenham shortly after passing the entrance to Pensthorpe Wildfowl Centre. This is open throughout the year and is well worth a visit. Fakenham itself is a pleasant enough town full of antique and small independent shops. It also has a good market and auctions, both held on Thursdays.

The bus, now numbered 29, continued towards Wells. We passed the magnificent Tudor-built East Barsham Manor, once set on the pilgrims' trail to Walsingham. Suddenly, the countryside changed and it became more hilly than you usually expect in Norfolk. As we approached Walsingham, you could catch glimpses of the Abbey ruins.

Walsingham Abbey

I spent a brief while in Walsingham whilst the bus continued its journey to Wells and began its return. This was far too little time to do such a place justice. Even when the museum and crypt are closed, you can, for a small fee, enjoy the grounds and ruins; a most idyllic spot.

The return to Fakenham was punctual, so I was able to catch the 9 to Holt. Holt is one of my favourite towns in the whole country. There is so much to enjoy, especially the antique shops. It was Christmas time and the shops were all hung with white lights. It was a real treat.

> **Alternative:** With more time, or a different plan, you can catch a service 46 bus from Fakenham to Holt via Blakeney. Several buses run most days about an hour and a half apart, allowing for a pleasant break in Blakeney.

Now, I needed to take the short journey to Sheringham before boarding a double-decker to Norwich. As you drop down into Sheringham, you pass Sheringham Park (National Trust), which is open all year for woodland walks. Upper Sheringham is typically North Norfolk - flint walls and red phone-boxes. The buses pull in beside the railway station and I had just enough time to buy a sandwich before continuing on my way. The last bus of the day was the only one to be late arriving. It was very crowded in Norwich and the Simonds service 2 bus has to run through as far as the station before making its return. This proved a more direct route than my journey from Diss earlier in the day. As it was now dark, I was glad of that.

Expedition 15: From Sudbury, across Essex to Finchingfield (Tuesdays, Fridays & Saturdays only)

Bus 236: Sudbury to Haverhill: 50 minutes
Bus 18: Haverhill to Saffron Walden: 33 minutes
Bus 17: Saffron Walden to Finchingfield: 35 minutes
Bus 16: Finchingfield to Chelmsford: 1 hour 10 minutes
Bus 70 or 71: Chelmsford to Colchester: 1 hour 45/25 minutes
Bus 753: Colchester to Sudbury: 50 minutes
(Alternatively, leave the service 70 at Braintree and catch either a 21 or 89 to Halstead, followed by an 11 or 13 to Sudbury. This sounds complicated, but buses are frequent, the route is more attractive and can even work out quicker.)

I had travelled along the 236 route before and knew well that Long Melford, Cavendish and Clare are all worthy of more attention. However, I had some distance to travel and couldn't stop this time.

Alternatives: You find, travelling this route, you follow a number of old abandoned railway lines. Though most are not strictly designated footpaths, in combination with other tracks, you can enjoy walks between Clare, Stoke-by-Clare and Wixoe. This 236 bus route links all these villages (Use O.S. Explorer map 210).
Or (Using O.S. Explorer map 196) walk from Long Melford to Lavenham returning to Sudbury on the 753, which runs hourly.

The timetable seems overly optimistic to assume this route can be covered in 50 minutes. We didn't hang about, but we were slightly late arriving at Haverhill and I only just caught my next bus. This was the service 18, a slightly different route from the one I'd taken to Saffron Walden the previous time. It was Tuesday - market-day in Saffron Walden and we picked up a fair number of passengers along the way. I left the bus at the common as we came into the town. From there you can walk to the top of the hill and see the castle, sadly in a dangerously crumbling condition. I had a couple of hours to spend there and that was no bad thing. There is a lot to see and do, even in winter. At the lower, older end of town, by the bridge are the superb Bridge End Gardens. The shops include a large number of small independent businesses, as a result of which you find things there you might not find elsewhere. State-of-the-art toilets are to be found in the Town Hall.

Saffron Walden castle ruins

Saffron Walden

This trip can only be enjoyed in its entirety on Tuesday, Friday and Saturday as the village link bus 17 only runs on those days. You catch it most easily at the foot of Common Hill on the side of the Common. It runs through a number of small attractive villages before ambling into that Essex gem that is Finchingfield. Beloved of biscuit-tin manufacturers, Finchingfield is a delightful village in every way. It shouts to have photos taken of it. Also, the bus-stop is situated beside a comfortable pub, The Fox.

Finchingfield

Having enjoyed lunch, there was just time to investigate the antique centre next door before catching the 16 service to Chelmsford. This takes you through Felstead and on into Chelmsford. The service terminates at the Retail Market, but if you stay aboard, you will be transported down to the Bus-Station.

Here, I discovered my brand-new timetable was already out of date. The 352 service to Halstead had largely disappeared and I found an alternative in the revamped 70 service which runs twice an hour between Chelmsford, Braintree and Colchester. At the beginning of this description, I offer two ways of making one's way back to Sudbury. As it was getting dark, I opted for the simpler one, but as I show, the alternative via Halstead has its advantages.

Had it been earlier in the day, I could have jumped off at Coggeshall and spent a while there. This is another place with much to recommend it - antique shops and historic buildings everywhere. The village website offers information about places to visit and walks around Coggeshall. Limited visiting to two National Trust properties is possible: Grange Barn and Paycocke's.

The final part of my journey was easy. It involved a short wait in Colchester before catching the 753 to Sudbury.

Expedition 16: A windy walk - From Melton to the Suffolk coast and circling back via Leiston & Saxmundham.

Bus 64: Melton to Aldringham: 46 minutes
Bus 165: Aldringham to Thorpeness: 6 minutes
Walk to Sizewell (3 miles), then to Leiston (1½ miles)
Bus 196: Leiston to Yoxford, then on to Saxmundham: 50 minutes
Bus 64: Saxmundham to Melton: 31 minutes

Melton is a good starting point. If you are driving there, parking is easy. Plenty of buses stop outside Melton Chapel. Since I first tried this route, bus routes have changed. The 165 used to take you directly to Thorpeness. Now you need to use a service 64 and change buses near the quaintly named 'Parrot & Punchbowl Inn', an old smugglers' pub of some antiquity. Then it is just a short run down to Thorpeness.

> **Alternative:** You might choose to ignore the rest of this expedition and instead stay on the 165 as far as Snape. There is plenty to see and do, and you can find all kinds of refreshment there. By reference to O.S. Explorer map 212, you can walk the 'sailor's path' to Aldeburgh. There will be no shortage of buses to return you to Melton.

Thorpeness

The area between Aldeburgh and Thorpeness is fascinating and full of wildlife. I arrived in Thorpeness to some frenzied activity. Overnight, the cargo of a timber ship, lost overboard a fortnight earlier had washed up on the beach, and builders and fishermen were salvaging planks as fast as they could before the sea reclaimed it all.

The walk from there to Sizewell follows the coastline, occasionally at beach level; the rest of the time along a low sandy cliff. It was a cool blustery January day but the wind was largely behind me, and the sun shone brightly all day. I had chosen to take this route from this direction as it allowed me more time for the walk, though it is quite feasible to work this journey the other way round. I also knew that on reaching Sizewell, I'd find the beach café open and I'd be ready for an 'all-day breakfast'.

The inner man satisfied, I made for Leiston along the road out of Sizewell. Most buses leaving Leiston pass along Main Street, where, opposite the library, I caught the minibus that plies the 196 route. I was only too pleased to be catching the one that goes via Dunwich. This was a route I'd used before. It also takes in the attractive villages of Middleton, Westleton and Darsham. The driver knew most of the passengers, who seemed to be regular users of this route.

I think I was the only passenger left by the time we reached Yoxford. From there, it was a short run along the road to Saxmundham.

> **Alternative:** You can get off at Yoxford and spend an hour or so enjoying the shops and galleries of Yoxford. Again, refreshments in cafes and pubs can be found here. Yoxford is, of course, a good place to catch the 521 service to Halesworth and Aldeburgh.

I had only a short time in Saxmundham before my route 64 bus arrived. This would carry me back to Melton, where my day had begun. This bus does pass through the small town of Wickham Market. Here is another place where it is easy to while away an hour or so and find the obligatory coffee and cake. A number of buses pass through the town, all stopping in the centre. Unlike some places where it can be confusing to the irregular traveller exactly where to catch a bus, there is no such problem here.

On one occasion, I took my dog on this trip. She thoroughly enjoyed it and was entirely welcome aboard the buses we used.

Expedition 17: From Stowmarket, around the lanes of Suffolk to Ipswich and back (Tues or Thurs only)

Bus 461: Stowmarket to Bildeston: 32 minutes
Bus 111: Bildeston to Ipswich: 52 minutes
Bus 70: Ipswich to Woodbridge and on to Ipswich: 1 hour 43 minutes
Bus 113: Ipswich to Stoke Ash: 53 minutes
Bus 456: Stoke Ash to Stowmarket: 29 minutes

There are quicker ways of covering all these journeys, but that wasn't really the point. Bildeston isn't a bad route to take. Buses connect very well there, so you don't spend long waiting between buses. Also, the views of the Suffolk countryside in summer can be quite spectacular. Since there are now fewer service buses operating between Stowmarket and Bildeston, you need to plan this trip for a Tuesday or a Thursday.

> **Alternative:** Increasingly, dial-up bus services are being introduced to cover the more rural areas. The area between Stowmarket and Hadleigh is covered by Optua Community Transport (01449 616000) and Hadleigh Communtity Transport (01473 826242). This opens up all kinds of opportunities when regular services don't meet one's needs.

Even more splendid is the journey from Ipswich to Woodbridge and back. It takes nearly two hours and bus drivers tend to be a little surprised that anyone should want to remain aboard without apparently getting anywhere. The villages you pass through are delightful - Grundisburgh, Charsfield, Dallinghoo, Bredfield; all before you reach Woodbridge. Then it is on to Great and Little Bealings and Playford, returning at length to Ipswich Bus Station, which admittedly is less than beautiful.

A friend who happens to be blind accompanied me on this journey. We left his dog at home on this occasion. It was a pleasant day and there was enough time between buses to stop for refreshment.

There must be plenty of people who regularly travel from Ipswich to Stowmarket. It can be be a bit monotonous. If so, why not consider the way we returned to Stowmarket

The 113 service from Ipswich heads towards Diss in Norfolk. Along that route is Stoke Ash White Horse, which also happens to be on one of the routes from Diss to Stowmarket (456). The twenty-minute gap between the two buses affords time for a swift pint. They were running bang on time as usual, and we arrived home, having gone from Ipswich to Stowmarket in an hour and forty minutes, allowing for refreshment halfway.

Expedition 18: From Manningtree to the seaside and back by way of Constable Country

Bus 2: Manningtree to Clacton: 49 minutes
Bus 17A: Clacton to Point Clear: 24 minutes
Bus 17 (or 17A or 18): Point Clear to St. Osyth: 8 minutes
Bus 74: St. Osyth to Colchester: 38 minutes
Bus 247 (or 87 [sat]): Colchester to Dedham: 34 (or 39) minutes
Then walk via Flatford Mill to East Bergholt
Bus 96 (or 745): East Bergholt to Manningtree: 12 (or 32) minutes

I worked this trip on a warm Saturday in July. If travelling on a Saturday, do check your timetables, as services are not necessarily the same as for the rest of the week. I could have started and ended this trip at East Bergholt. The 93C from Ipswich to Mistley passes East Bergholt High school and gets you to Manningtree in plenty of time for the Clacton bus.

Manningtree, however, is a good place to travel from. Parking is easy and free. The trip across to Clacton is pleasant, carrying you via the villages of Little Bromley and Tendring, before entering the Clacton sprawl via the Factory Shopping Village. Once in Clacton, you find most buses start and terminate from Pier Avenue, a stone's throw from the sea. I was particularly taken with the gardens above the promenade (pictured below).

Nice day though it was, I was not remaining long. Buses to Point Clear and back run twice an hour.

> **Alternative:** You can easily reach other seaside towns from here - Walton & Frinton (buses 7 & 8), and Jaywick (buses 131 & 12).

Point Clear is a strange place. If sea-levels ever rise as far as they threaten to do, a number of the houses will disappear. The bus takes you to the entrance of a large holiday village. Walk another three-quarters of a mile and in Summer you can catch a ferry to Brightlingsea, making this part of a bus-trip circuit.

I returned to St. Osyth to find the Priory swathed in scaffolding. Hence the lack of photograph. Instead, I was quite taken with the old village lock-up that had once hosted a witch before her hanging in 1582.

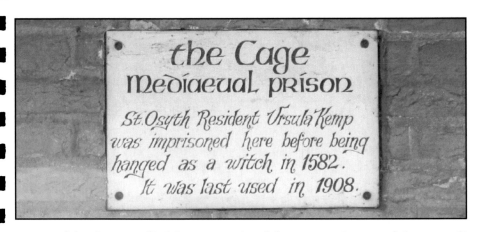

the Cage
mediaeval prison

St. Osyth Resident Ursula Kemp
was imprisoned here before being
hanged as a witch in 1582.
It was last used in 1908.

My bus to Colchester arrived bang on time and I was off through Wivenhoe and the campus of Essex University. I took time out to enjoy a cheese scone and a cup of coffee at the Minories, just behind Colchester Bus-Station.

The Minories, near Colchester bus station

The trip to Dedham divides itself into two. You seem to be interminably wending your way out of Colchester; then suddenly you are into countryside, in and out of Ardleigh and heading for Dedham. This really is one of the jewels of East Anglia. There are craft workshops, places to eat and drink and a place on the river where you can hire boats. The village is lovely, if a little crowded (but after all, it was a warm Saturday in July).

Now came the best part of the day. The area around Dedham is a sea of footpaths, most of which make for the River Stour and Flatford Mill. It helps to have a map (O.S. Explorer map 196) but even if you forget it, if you pick a warm Saturday in Summer there will be plenty of other walkers to point you in the right direction.

Alternative: When or wherever you reach the River Stour, you can choose to continue walking in an easterly direction all the way back to Manningtree. The wildlife along there is spectacular.

Flatford Mill

Leaving Flatford Mill behind, East Bergholt is about another mile away. This is another lovely village with a great collection of old buildings and an unusual bell-cage beside the church where the bells are rung at ground level (see below).

If in doubt as to where to catch buses (and the descriptions in the timetable aren't awfully helpful), look for the old Lambe School, now a village hall, just downhill from the church and shop. Bus-stops aren't very obvious in East Bergholt (I expect they detract from the decor), but they don't really need them. The buses seem to stop for anyone who puts a hand out. I was soon winging my way back to Manningtree, where I'd started, about seven hours earlier.

The small town of Eye lies on route 456 between Stowmarket and Diss, route 482 between Diss and Laxfield, and routes 113 & 114 between Ipswich and Diss

Ely Cathedral is easily reached by service 12 from Cambridge or Newmarket

Henstead Tropical Garden, open a number of times during the year, lies close to route 523, between Southwold & Beccles

Expedition 19: From Stowmarket, taking a tour around North and Central Suffolk

Bus 458: Stowmarket to Diss: 60 minutes
Bus 482: Diss to Stradbroke: 38 minutes
Bus 482: Stradbroke to Laxfield: 9 minutes
Bus 121: Laxfield to Halesworth: 24 minutes
Bus 588: Halesworth to Bungay: 28 minutes
Bus 580: Bungay to Diss: 42 minutes
Bus 456: Diss to Stowmarket: 50 minutes

To be honest, the journey I ended doing wasn't quite how I had planned it. but it all goes to show, it helps to have a plan B.

I had travelled to Diss from Stowmarket a number of times, but never along this route - the long way. It is certainly the most rural of rural rides, out through Mendlesham and Wickham Skeith before plodding across darkest Suffolk to Burgate. I swear there was grass growing in the middle of the road and it was barely wide enough for a single car, let alone a bus. Still, we made our way out to Wortham and Redgrave before heading for Diss bus-station - a circuitous route (the invention of a tortured mind?), but a lovely one.

From Diss to Stradbroke meant more rural deviations and I was deposited in the centre of the village around lunch-time. It was Tuesday, which means music-day at the Queen's Head. Guitarists, harpists and squeezers of assorted boxes gather there every Tuesday afternoon to entertain themselves and other people. It's a great way to spend an hour or two.

Eventually, I left them to it and headed back up to the church to catch my 482 bus to Laxfield. Stradbroke and Laxfield lie about 5 miles apart and are very similar in many ways. Both have a fine church, an ancient village street and a couple of good pubs. Both once had many more shops, as is clear from the fronts of many buildings that are now houses.

Having arrived at Laxfield, in spite of apparently being in the right place early enough, I saw no sign of the bus I had intended to catch.

My original plan had been...
Bus 100: (Tuesday or Friday) Laxfield to Harleston
Bus 580: Harleston to Diss
Bus 456: Diss to Stowmarket

In the absence of the 100 bus, I had to rethink. The first bus to arrive was the 121 which passes in the opposite direction towards Halesworth four days a week. There wasn't a lot of choice. It meant a longer journey, but I knew I could get home via Bungay, so I hopped aboard.

I usually carry several timetables with me, so I wasn't completely in the dark. The rest of the trip was old territory for me. I'd used the same route home from Halesworth on at least one occasion before. It was a fortuitous change of plan as I found a real bargain in one of Bungay's many antique shops. Such are the joys of bus-travel.

Since that time, changes have been made to timetables and should you try this route, you may find you arrive back in Diss too late for the last bus to Stowmarket. You'll have to part with a bit of money for your travel, but the hourly train service will whisk you back to Stowmarket in less than fifteen minutes.

Expedition 20: From Bury to Cromer and back

Bus - Whippet service B: Bury to Cromer: about 2 hours 15 minutes in each direction

From Spring until nearly Christmas, Whippet Coaches of Swavesey, Cambridge run a series of services across East Anglia that head for seaside destinations. You can pick up leaflets at Tourist Information Centres (TICs). They accept bus-passes. To ensure your seats are reserved, you can book any number of people for a booking fee of just £2 at any TIC. You need to book. Coaches may by-pass towns on the route where no-one has registered an interest.

I chose to travel from Bury to Cromer. Others travelling with me got off at Norwich or Sheringham. This coach also makes pick-ups in Haverhill and Diss. The coaches used on these routes are generally modern and comfortable.

We left Bury a little late, but as there were no customers booked to be picked up at Diss, we headed the quicker way to Norwich by way of Thetford and the A11. It was a fine Autumn day and the route proved to be an attractive one. Norwich is always a bit of a nightmare for traffic and it took us some time before we were off on the Cromer road. However, you get a good tour of much of historic Norwich on this route so I just sat back and enjoyed it.

Nearly to Cromer, we turned up past Felbrigg Hall and on to Sheringham. This was the stopping point for some. I, however, was bound for Cromer.

> **Alternative:** There are several bus routes linking Sheringham and Cromer, so there is no reason why, with your bus-pass, you should not spend part of your day in each place before picking up the coach to return home. Sheringham has a steam railway that runs most of the way to Holt. There might be time to enjoy this as part of your day out.

The coach parked right beside toilets and only a short distance from town and sea-front. There is a good deal to recommend Cromer. I headed for the pier and a sandwich and coffee lunch. The new Rocket House Cafe is also very good. Both offer spectacular views.

©Will Black Photography

There are plenty of gift shops and other opportunities to part with your money. I was attracted to the town's three second-hand bookshops. The small museum beside the church is well worth a visit, but if you just want a leisurely look at the sights, in summer there are horse and carriage trips round the town and a 'train' that operates along the promenade.

On this occasion, we had something under four hours to enjoy. It was over all too soon and we made pretty much the same journey in reverse. Passing through Norwich this time, however, we saw Tombland and the Cathedral Close, as we followed a slightly different route from before.

This is just one of several trips on offer described as Whippet Coastal Services. I came away thinking I was certainly going to try some of the others.

Expedition 21: From Stowmarket to Clacton and back

Bus - Whippet service E: Stowmarket to Clacton: 60 minutes
Bus 8 (or 7): Clacton to Frinton: 25 minutes
Walk to Walton
Bus 105: Walton Station to Colchester: 52 minutes
Bus 93: Colchester to Ipswich: 1 hour 13 minutes
Bus 87 (or 88): Ipswich to Stowmarket: 41 minutes

Using one of Whippet Coaches' coastal trips to reach Clacton, I found it easy to find a different route back. For half the year, service E runs three days a week. The journey there was quick, comfortable and efficient. It was also unspectacular, following main roads most of the way.

I told the driver not to expect me for the return journey, and caught the first bus I could to Frinton. These come about every half hour (services 7 & 8). The route is mostly close to the coast and you might choose to stop at Holland-on-sea. I got off at the railway gates at Frinton and walked down Connaught Drive to the sea front. There is something a bit special about walking the full two miles to

Walton-on-the-Naze along the top of the cliff, on grass. On a fine day in summer, the sea at Frinton is as good as anywhere for bathing as it is shallow and the water heats up quickly.

The greensward at Frinton

This however was a chilly day in October and I was content merely to look at the sea instead. My next bus departed from the Rail Station at Walton, which is easy enough to find. This bus arrived bang on time and I enjoyed a pleasant run through the flat lands of that part of Essex on my way to Colchester.

I had the best part of an hour in Colchester before my departure for Ipswich. There is plenty to see without having to walk too far from the bus-station... the Castle, Natural History Museum and Hollytrees museum are all within a five minute walk.

A sign adorns the 'Temporary Bus-Station' in Colchester. It is dated 2006 and wonders just how long does something have to be the way it is before it can no longer be described as temporary.

I thought the journey to Ipswich was supposed to be reasonably direct according to the timetable I had. But it ambled through most of the villages of East Anglia before finally deciding Ipswich was where it was bound. Then, all I needed was the first bus back to Stowmarket to complete a satisfactory and successful day.

Expedition 22: From Martlesham to Snape and Aldeburgh

Bus 165: Martlesham to Snape Maltings: 34 minutes
Bus 165: Snape to Aldeburgh: 12 minutes
Bus 64: Aldeburgh to Martlesham: 1 hour 18 minutes

When I give my lectures on travelling by bus-pass, I emphasise the value of out-of-town bus stops. Martlesham Water Bridge is a good place to catch a bus. Plenty of buses pass that way and you can park for nothing all day nearby. I could have started from home in Stowmarket and come to this point via Ipswich. In other words, this could have been a longer trip and might have been started from anywhere that is only a bus ride away from Ipswich. The 165 service runs hourly through the middle of the day and the route from Martlesham is an attractive one.

If you do as I did, you may be tempted to board a 64 bus which is scheduled to pass that way a few minutes earlier, and change at Woodbridge. However, that service goes all round the houses to reach the Turban Centre in Woodbridge and you may find it arrives after the 165 has left.

The 165 runs you straight into Woodbridge past the station and the Tide Mill. Then as it leaves Woodbridge, you cross the river at Wilford Bridge and head for what is now almost a new town at Rendlesham, close to the old Bentwaters Air Base. Look out for the gateway to Campsea Ashe Priory (see right).

Through Tunstall, you journey on through Blaxhall, past the Youth Hostel and some open lands towards Snape. The Maltings are visible from some distance.

Once there, there is plenty to occupy visitors who want to fill two or three hours before their next bus. From Easter, there are river trips up the Alde. There are magnificent walks both sides of the river. You can pick up a leaflet about them from the information point or the R.S.P.B. office there. You will find shops, galleries and places to eat. I had a superb hot bacon sandwich in the cafe run by Metfield Bakery.

Alternative: You might consider circling back from Snape using a different set of buses:-
Bus 165: Snape to Leiston: 30 minutes (schooldays only)
Then either...
Bus 64: Leiston to Martlesham: 68 minutes
or taking the scenic route...
Bus 165: Snape to Melton, Bus 63: Melton to Framlingham
Bus 481: Framlingham to Saxmundham, Bus 64: back to Martlesham

I chose to move on to Aldeburgh, eventually returning from there. The 64 service runs approximately hourly back to Woodbridge and Ipswich.

Aldeburgh is a splendid place to find yourself, winter or summer. My stop on this occasion was short, however, and before long I was aboard a 64 bus heading back to where I'd started. This route, like a number, passes through the pleasant little town of Wickham Market. Here, you might get off and make the most of an excellent teashop and antique shop whilst awaiting the next bus. There is no shortage of buses heading from there to Woodbridge and beyond.

Expedition 23: From Newmarket to Bishops Stortford and back

Bus 12: Newmarket to Cambridge: 37 minutes
Bus 26: Cambridge to Royston: 40 minutes
Bus 331: Royston to Ware: 1 hour 6 minutes
Bus 351: Ware to Bishops Stortford: 46 minutes
Bus 301: Bishops Stortford to Saffron Walden: 40 minutes
Bus 7: Saffron Walden to Cambridge: 1 hour 9 minutes
Bus 11: Cambridge to Newmarket: 38 minutes

Planning a route like this, it is well worth checking you have all the latest bus timetables. A good way to make sure is to use the website www.traveline.org.uk, which enables you to also print off local maps showing you where in a town the bus-stops can be found.

I started from Newmarket because the buses from Cambridge run later there than they do to Bury St. Edmunds. As it happened, I needn't have worried. All my connections were made with ease, and I arrived back exactly when I had planned.

I caught my first bus of the day from the stop beside the Horseracing Museum in Newmarket. It was about ten minutes late and the driver was clearly intent on making up for lost time.

It must have been about the quickest bus trip I've ever been on, and sure enough there was no problem over catching the next bus to Royston.

The statue on the roundabout just outside Newmarket

The 26 bus leaves Cambridge by way of the Botanical Gardens and passes through some attractive villages - Harston, Foxton and Melbourn - where a number of thatched cottages sit amidst far newer houses. At one point we passed close to the Shepreth Wildlife Park. The bus takes you into Royston town centre before continuing as far as the Tesco supermarket. The next bus could be caught from either place.

It was only a short wait before the 331 bus to Ware arrived. This took us into the Hertfordshire countryside, where the flatter lands of Cambridgeshire were replaced by gently rolling hills. We climbed up and across open farmland before plunging down into a series of interesting villages. At Barley, the pub sign for the Fox and Hounds stretched right across the road. One minute we seemed to be up on top of the world, another moment, tumbling down to some small town or village. We passed through Buntingford and Puckeridge before making for the town of Ware.

Alternative: Had I chosen to travel a little later, I would have needed to change buses at Puckeridge instead and catch the 386 to Bishops Stortford, missing Ware entirely.

I quite like Ware. There is a river and a canal, complete with narrow-boats. It is well connected by bus and train routes. If you

Ware

have time it is well worth exploring. The 331 bus I was using continued as far as the historic town of Hertford, but as I had planned to visit there another day (and another way), I left Hertford to another occasion (see expedition 27).

You catch the 351 bus to Saffron Walden from just outside the college, close to the town centre. This part of the journey is really fascinating. The route takes you through a number of rather elegant up-market villages. Yes, there really is a place called Much Hadham (and a Little Hadham). Over rivers and streams, the road winds its way past a succession of impressive houses before entering the town of Bishops Stortford.

I must admit I was a little disappointed with Bishops Stortford. Like many towns, its old riverside area is in the process of being developed and will probably look a bit better some time in the future. But the overall impression is of a place a little down-at-heel. Castle Park is nice, but you are not enormously aware of the 'historic town' it claims to be.

Saffron Walden is not very far away, but the 301 bus route makes it seem like miles. This is another of those ambling routes such as only a rural bus company could dream up, visiting villages barely identifiable by map, as if in an attempt to delay passengers from discovering one of Essex's best kept secrets; by which I mean Saffron Walden.

> **Alternative:** One of the first places you pass on leaving Bishops Stortford is Stansted. Here you may visit the reconstructed site of Mountfitchet Castle or the 'House on the hill Toy Museum.' Visiting Stansted needs time and thus is not for a trip like this.

The meandering journey led us through Ugley (certainly not ugly), Quendon, and in and out of Widdington, where the bus had to slow to a stop to allow a herd of deer to cross in front of us. At Newport, we passed the old toll-bridge and entered the quaintly named village, Wendens Ambo.

> **Alternative:** Just before you reach Saffron Walden, you pass close to the stately home of Audley End (now in the care of English Heritage) - a place to make time to visit.

I have mentioned before the delights of Saffron Walden. There is a published Town Trail that takes in castle, church, a series of medieval houses and the lovely Bridge End garden.

My penultimate bus of the day arrived a little late - it was school closing time and the roads were choked with traffic. Still, the route 7 bus made good time as it headed for Cambridge and I was soon aboard my last bus and heading for Newmarket, just as the winter light was fading. As I've discovered before, it is amazing how far you can travel in a day with a bus pass.

Expedition 24: From Bury St. Edmunds to Long Melford and back

Bus 373: Bury St. Edmunds to Clare: 53 minutes
Bus 373 (or 236): Clare to Long Melford: 15 minutes
Bus 753: Long Melford to Bury St. Edmunds: 53 minutes

This is an afternoon trip that takes in some of the best parts of West Suffolk. The buses numbered 370-375 operate a number of different variations on a theme, linking Sudbury, Clare, Glemsford and Bury. Each day, Monday to Saturday in the early afternoon, a 373 bus runs from Bury to Clare before continuing on to Sudbury.

We left Bury on time, and wandered out past Horsecroft Hall towards Whepstead. Immediately, the countryside became less flat, more gently rolling as we moved in and out of a succession of small river valleys.

Whepstead is a village more or less divided in two. We took in both parts before moving out towards Rede. We passed the South Lodge at Stonecross Green, surely one of the prettiest houses in Suffolk. We then circled back, passing herds of deer to Brockley Green and on to Hartest, one of the loveliest villages I know. You plunge down to the Green in the centre of the village before rising up again and veering off in the direction of Hawkedon. As you approach the church, you skirt a lush river valley; then before you know it, the bus is carrying you further into this wonderful wilderness to Stansfield and Poslingford. At Poslingford, you pick up a stream and follow it all the way to Clare. Having run through the town to the Western end, the bus number changed and the bus was away again in the direction of Sudbury.

Make time to stay awhile in Clare. There is an old Priory, some interesting shops, a museum (open in Summer), an antique centre and an auction house. It is lovely to wander down along the River Stour or to climb the castle mound. You can pick up a town trail sheet from the Information Centre in the old railway station.

Cavendish

The route taken by this bus now passes through Cavendish, beloved by photographers and painters, but avoids Glemsford as it heads for Long Melford. You see the towers of Melford Hall from some way off. Here was where I was getting off. I like a little time in Long Melford, exploring the antique shops and galleries.

I timed my afternoon to allow the last journey of the day to be in daylight. It was still winter. The 753 usually operates with double-deckers. You get a great view of the countryside around Lavenham as you head towards, through and beyond. Lavenham, of course, is well worth exploring, but on this occasion I was heading back to Bury. We wandered off round Stanningfield and Whelnetham, before picking up the main road again and entering Bury just as daylight was fading.

It is easy to reach Bury from Newmarket, Diss, Stowmarket, Mildenhall, Thetford or Haverhill. So this could easily have been part of a longer journey that started and ended somewhere entirely different. The lovely villages of West Suffolk are a bit of a well-kept secret, so this trip is definitely one to savour.

Expedition 25: A circular tour around Suffolk

Bus 456: Stowmarket to Diss: 1 hour
Bus 580: Diss to Beccles: 1 hour 13 minutes
Bus 522: Beccles to Halesworth: 34 minutes
Bus 521: Halesworth to Saxmundham: 24 minutes
Bus 64: Saxmundham to Ipswich: 1 hour 14 minutes
Bus 87A: Ipswich to Stowmarket: 30 minutes

This is a good circular route that could be followed from any starting point around the circle. Alternatively, you might begin from places that are joined by other bus routes to places on this journey. For example, it would be easy to plan this route from Leiston, Bury St. Edmunds or Bildeston, to name just a few.

As most routes in Suffolk are aligned east-west, this expedition made use of two of the few north-south links, covered by bus routes 456/458 and 522/521.

It was the tail-end of winter when I set out, and a wet one at that. The 458 and 456 routes connecting Stowmarket and Diss follow narrow country roads and we splashed through deep puddles as we made our way. This proved to be a tortuous route. By the time we had been travelling for 45 minutes, a signpost showed we were still only nine miles from our starting point. But this is the joy of rural travel.

The first primroses were starting to cover the banks near Wickham Skeith and flocks of ducks and gulls were making the most of flooded fields.

The short wait at Diss (pictured left) gave me just time to stock up with provisions for the rest of the journey. Then it was away along the Waveney valley towards Beccles. This is a route I have used a number of times and it is always a delight. Fields alongside the river had become lakes, and swans were flocking in their numbers as we motored past Harleston towards Bungay.

You approach Beccles across flat water meadows, passing the the River Waveney as you enter the town. The Old Market Place, the town's Bus Station has public toilets and places to eat and drink only yards away.

> **Alternative:** In the recent past in Summer time, the Big Dog Ferry was a free ferry that took you up river to Geldeston Locks Inn, a pub more easily reached by boat than any other way. Until the ferry is re-established you might instead walk the riverbank path to the lock, stopping for lunch, then returning the same way or walking up the causeway to Geldeston and catching the next 580 bus to Beccles.

Beccles

The 522 and 521 services run from Beccles via Halesworth to Leiston and you might choose to travel the whole way. I found connections with Ipswich worked better if I changed at Saxmundham. It only left an eight minute gap between buses, but as they were running to time as usual, this was not a problem. The journey again is convoluted; the 522 taking half an hour to take us just six miles away from Beccles, but it is an attractive route in all seasons of the year. From Halesworth onwards, the 521 speeds up, following the A12 for much of the way. Then, with brief deviations for Darsham and Yoxford, we arrived mid-afternoon in Saxmundham near the railway bridge.

At this point it became necessary to cross over the road to catch the 64 bus to Ipswich. It seems to be taking you in the wrong direction, but soon circles round and makes for Wickham Market and Woodbridge. Finally, it is on to Ipswich where I changed buses at Tower Ramparts rather than going all the way to the bus station. This time it was an even tighter connection, but we made it with ease.

The 87A bus arrived just three minutes after I'd been dropped off and it was pleasant amble back to Stowmarket via Needham Market.

Expedition 26: A Wednesday trip - from Hoxne and back

Bus 497: Hoxne to Harleston: 26 minutes
Bus 498: Harleston to Halesworth: 37 minutes
Bus 522: Halesworth to Beccles: 37 minutes
Bus 580: Beccles to Diss: 1 hour 24 minutes
Then Bus 482: Diss to Hoxne: 24 minutes
or Bus 113: Diss to Brome: 10 min. **&** Bus 318: Brome to Hoxne: 12 min

This has to be a Wednesday trip as it uses two routes that only operate once a week. These are the first two buses of the day, which appear to be a tight connection until you realise they are actually the same bus and driver, with a change of number in between.

Imagine you live in the middle of nowhere but are fortunate enough to have a few buses pass through your village. Then, you have plenty of opportunity to go on an expedition. Hoxne is one such village, but far from being the only one you might use as a starting point. Others include Eyke, Bildeston, Sweffling, Occold, Wangford, Moulton etc. etc. In other words, buses are plentiful enough to enable expeditions to be planned from any number of out-of-the-way places and still get you home in time for tea.

Wingfield Castle

The 497 route from Hoxne heads north through Wingfield, past the castle and close to the old monastic college. Then you follow the Suffolk side of the Waveney valley before plunging down past the lakes at Weybread and on into Harleston. Harleston is an attractive small town, far enough away from other places to maintain its individuality. However, on this ocasion, there was no time to stop.

I began the second leg of my journey on the same bus, now a 498, following a route that found the centre of remarkably few villages. Apart from Fressingfield, it was as if the route was avoiding most other places. We did pick up a handful of passengers, but I felt I was there to keep the driver company, so to speak.

Having reached Halesworth, the rest of the day can be organised in a variety of ways as you can use buses that run several times during the day and stops along the way can be allowed for. I have explored Halesworth on several occasions. It has a lot to recommend it. As a town, it is compact and has a good variety of small independent shops. The Cut, the local theatre venue also offers refreshment throughout the day.

Bus stops in Halesworth are easily negotiated. Virtually all buses stop at Saxons Way, close to the centre (also close to toilets).

The 522 begins to head straight along the main road towards Beccles, but after Spexhall, plunges into the wilds of nowhere and explores the more exotic corners of Westhall and Ringsfield before rediscovering its original purpose and, as if by accident, finds where it was meant to be going.

Beccles is worthy of some exploration. The museum at the top of the town has some splendid exhibits and the riverside, especially in summer is well worth investigating. From here, of course, you can travel by bus in a number of directions - to Southwold, Lowestoft, Norwich or Great Yarmouth as well as towards Diss, where I was heading. Boat trips are also available in summer. On this occasion however, there was just time to grab a coffee and excellent cheese scone at Farriers (beside the Bus Station) before moving on.

The 580 route along the Waveney valley is one I've used a lot. On this occasion, it visited a few additional villages. On leaving Bungay, we wandered round Denton and Alburgh before following the usual route to Harleston and Diss. Now, however, this ocasional deviation from the route has been scrapped.

As my connection with the 482 was tight, I got off the bus a stop before the bus station, giving me a couple of extra minutes to ensure I caught the next bus back to Hoxne.

Along the Waveney Valley

Alternative: If you miss the connection or you want longer in Diss, on schooldays there is another option. Catch the 113 bus bound for Ipswich and get off at Brome as soon as you've crossed the A140. You then have about 25 minutes to wait for the 318. As you've got a bit of time, and the road is fairly quiet, you can walk down as far as Brome Street and wait for your bus by the village hall. That will take you back to Hoxne.

Expedition 27: From Sudbury to Hertford and back

Bus 12: Sudbury to Halstead: 44 minutes

Bus 21: Halstead to Braintree: 35 minutes

Bus 70: Braintree to Chelmsford: 42 minutes

Bus 59: Chelmsford to Harlow: 51 minutes

Bus 524: Harlow to Hertford: 24 minutes

Bus 324: Hertford to Broxbourne railway station: 21 minutes

Train fom Broxbourne to Cambridge: 59 minutes

Bus 13: Cambridge to Haverhill: 57 minutes

Bus 236: Haverhill to Sudbury (not Saturday): 50 minutes

It goes without saying that this is a long trip and not for the faint-hearted. It helps to start early. I began just before 9:00 a.m. and that was not really early enough. There are two earlier buses you might take.

> **Alternative:** You may have more time at the end if you do this trip the other way round. Buses from Halstead to Sudbury run a good bit later than those from Haverhill to Sudbury.

In the end, I didn't quite make it all the way round through reasons beyond my control - such is travel, however you plan it.

The first leg is a pleasant enough journey. You leave Sudbury by way of Ballingdon Hill and circle around Bulmer and a number of attractive surrounding villages. As you leave Bulmer and head for Gestingthorpe, on the right you may catch sight of what looks like a castle ruin. That is exactly what you were intended to believe. It is an old folly built in the grounds of Belchamp Hall.

As you motor on, you pass substantial village greens at Gestingthorpe and Wickham St. Paul. The tiny, almost circular church at Little Maplestead is passed twice as the tortuous route winds up hill and down dale. Finally, you rejoin the main road and enter Halstead.

Halstead remains a small bustling town owing to its never having been by-passed. In the eighteenth-century Townsford Mill, which straddles the River Colne, you will find a splendid antiques centre. There is also a nearby river walk.

Halstead

The next part of the journey is unremarkable, taking you slowly to Braintree, then towards the outskirts of Chelmsford and on to the bus station. From there, the first part of the journey to Harlow becomes more interesting. You leave Chelmsford much more rapidly and trek through a succession of villages mostly called 'something' Roding. Then, after the spreading greens of Hatfield Heath, you make for Harlow.

Alternative: Approaching Harlow you pass the Gibberd Garden. Open from April to September, it is a lovely water garden filled with sculptures and is well worth a look if you can make the time.

Harlow is reached through the old town, before you encounter the Harlow you expect and rather dread. The bus station is modern and serviceable and offers a range of facilities.

Two bus routes link Harlow with Hertford. I chose the 524 as it came sooner, but the 724 is equally efficient. The advantage of new towns is they are designed with traffic in mind. We were out of Harlow in an instant and on our way towards Ware. It soon became evident that something rather terrible was wrong with our bus. It was horribly low at the rear and bounced alarmingly over every bump in the road. It didn't seem to bother our driver who carried on regardless, and we arrived at Hertford on time, if a little battered.

Hertford is a fine town. It seems to be everything Harlow is not. I enjoyed wandering round the castle grounds and with more time to spare would have enjoyed exploring further. But finding myself now at my greatest distance from home, I needed to keep moving.

Hertford

I could have returned the way I had come, or gone by way of Chelmsford to Colchester before making for Sudbury. But I wanted to find a more interesting alternative, so I headed for Cambridge.

This meant using a train. At the time of writing, this cost me a little over £11. The bus to Broxbourne station dropped me off bang on time, but whereas buses had served me well all day, the train was half an hour late. This meant I had to rethink the end to my journey.

Alternative: Broxbourne station is situated beside the Lea (or Lee) Valley Walk (See book by Leigh Hatts), a glorious watery amble that covers over 50 miles from near Luton to London's East-end. Another day, another time, this looked quite appealing.

When the train did arrive, it gave me a pleasant and comfortable journey to Cambridge. You have such respect for the railway builders of the past: we seemed to cross endless watery places that should have defied any kind of construction.

Outside Cambridge station, you find buses to the city centre come every five minutes. You need them, as it is quite a walk. Get off outside the John Lewis store. Drummer Street Bus Station is only a short distance away.

My lost time with the train meant I could not get back to Sudbury via Haverhill that day, so I had to replan my schedule. The alternative could have involved another train, but I chose to head for Bury St. Edmunds using Bus Route 12. Even then, I could not get back to Sudbury that night, so I caught the last bus back to Stowmarket where I live, leaving my car in a car park in Sudbury overnight to be picked up the next morning. (Getting from Stowmarket to Sudbury can require a slightly convoluted plan involving demand-responsive vehicles - see www.traveline.org.uk)

Expedition 28: Garboldisham to Norwich & back via Thetford

Bus 66 (Thursday only): Garboldisham to Norwich: 41 minutes
Bus 727 (National Express): Norwich to Thetford: 1 hour
Bus 332: Thetford to Bury: 52 minutes
Bus 338: Bury to Garboldisham: 1 hour 8 minutes

There are countless ways to get to Norwich. Several once-a-week bus routes exist from places in Suffolk. This one only works on a Thursday, but it is an expedition that could equally well have started and finished in Stanton, Hepworth, Barningham or Hopton.

From Garboldisham, the route passes through the pleasant small town of East Harling and out via Attleborough towards Norwich. At Snetterton, you pass one of the largest rookeries I've seen, but otherwise, the journey is unspectacular. The bus leaves you beside the John Lewis store.

Norwich has a host of attractions and there is nothing I like more than exploring the shops, museums and hidden corners of the city. This time, however, I would not be staying long. I had already planned a different way back.

> **Alternative:** You could miss Norwich out altogether and stop awhile at Attleborough instead. The National Express 727 coach I subsequently caught from Norwich stopped in the centre of Attleborough, en-route to Thetford.

What I was pleasantly surprised to discover was that there are occasions when you can use your bus-pass on a National Express coach. There is no regular bus service operating between Thetford and Norwich. This being the case, provided there is room on board, one of the two National Express services (727) will accept bus-passes and allow you to travel between those places. I have yet to discover just how many other journeys in East Anglia can be made this way.

The 727 coach from Norwich to the three London airports is comfortable and reliable, running ten times a day. In under an hour we were pulling into Thetford Bus Station.

Thetford has a lot of history tucked not very far below its modern surface. There is a lovely priory and two fine museums, as well as walks along river banks. Even on this occasion there was time for a short amble.

Two services operate between Bury St. Edmunds and Thetford. There is even a third way (201 & 193) via Brandon. But the best for me is the 332 route which meanders around the villages of Livermere and Ampton, Ingham and Culford, crossing streams and passing lakes. Ampton Water

Ampton Water

pictured here is only a short walk away from the bus route.

> **Alternative:** If you have time, leave the bus near Great Livermere church and walk around the lake, which is an absolute haven for wildlife. This is one of the loveliest and least known parts of Suffolk. Another bus will be along in 2 hours.

Along the way, we were treated to small clusters of roe deer and spring flowers emerging in the woods and along the verges. Arriving at Bury in what was still mid-afternoon, there was time for tea and cake (there is no shortage of good places to find such delights). Then, I was climbing aboard my last bus of the day, the 338 bound for Garboldisham. This route heads out into the countryside of north Suffolk, passing Ixworth before making for Stanton and a succession of smaller places before terminating just over the border in Norfolk where my day had begun.

Expedition 29: From Bury to Hunstanton and back another way

Bus 11: Bury to Cambridge: 1 hour 12 minutes
Whippet coach C: Cambridge to Hunstanton: 1 hour 45 minutes
Bus 35: Hunstanton to Kings Lynn: 35 minutes
Bus X1: Kings Lynn to Swaffham: 32 minutes
Bus X1: Swaffham to East Dereham: 33 minutes
Bus 11: East Dereham to Watton: 25 minutes
Bus 81: Watton to Thetford: 45 minutes
Bus 84: Thetford to Bury: 30 minutes

As I've already shown, throughout the summer months, Whippet Coaches run seaside trips across East Anglia. In order to join the Hunstanton coach, I needed to reach Cambridge before 9:30 a.m.

Bury St. Edmunds is probably the best place in East Anglia to use as a base for bus-pass travel. Regular service routes radiate out in at least a dozen directions directions, carrying you into all parts of the region on a single bus. It is just unfortunate that there is no direct link with Ipswich.

The early morning buses into Cambridge used to catch the worst of the traffic. The re-designing of the timetable has sorted this out. We sailed into Cambridge soon after nine o'clock without a hint of a hold-up.

The Whippet Coach to Hunstanton was there good and early and the few of us travelling that day were soon on our way, out across the fens and into Ely. The cathedral is visible from a long way off.

From there, the A10 is a busy little road and even on a good day, it is unlikely the bus would have been able to run to time. As it was, we hit problems. Just beyond Downham Market, we met a serious traffic jam. Try to avoid Kings Lynn on a friday. The roads in and out are a nightmare at the moment. By the time we had found our way into the centre and out again, we were at least half an hour late.

The coast road to Hunstanton was nearly as busy, but pleasant enough as we motored through the woodland around the Sandringham estate. At Heacham you pass fields of Lavender before turning into Hunstanton.

Hunstanton

Normally, I'd have remained there about four hours till the coach was scheduled to bring us back, but I was keen to see how easy it was to get home another way. Hunstanton is a seaside town with something for everyone. There is a good beach, plenty of eating places and a range of seaside amusements. It is small and appealing, especially the way the grassy centre tumbles toward the promenade.

I had planned my return route before I started out. There are many ways I might have made my way back to Bury St. Edmunds. You could catch the coasthopper bus and travel in an easterly direction to Sheringham or Cromer, then on to Norwich and back by a combination of buses and/or trains. The coasthopper as far as Wells will link up with buses to Fakenham and Norwich (see expedition 14). The simplest way back is by bus to Kings Lynn, then using the service 40, you'll reach Thetford or Brandon, from where there are buses to Bury.

> **Alternative:** If you are staying in the area, why not try this one... From Hunstanton, take the coasthopper bus to Wells, then follow the delightful route described next as Expedition 30.

I chose to catch a bus number 35 back to Kings Lynn Bus Station. From there the X1 runs through Norfolk via Norwich to Great Yarmouth and Lowestoft. This is a half-hourly service. I broke my journey from there to East Dereham in Swaffham.

Swaffham is a lovely little market town with space to wander, places to eat and a good assortment of shops. You'll find an excellent tea-room at the back of the second-hand bookshop.

The journey was pleasant, especially when we pulled away from the main roads and in and out of Narborough. The area is heavily wooded and full of wildlife. At one point I could see three buzzards soaring above the trees. You know you are near Swaffham when the wind generators become visible. You alight from the bus at the top of the market square. Swaffham on that occasion was relatively quiet.

After my short stay there, I waited for another X1 bus and headed for Dereham which was far busier and choked with traffic. I only just made my next connection.

> **Alternative:** If you are pushing time, you can get off the bus at the Millwrights pub at Toftwood and cross the road to await the Watton bus (service 11).

The road to Watton is a winding one through Shipdham (with its rather lovely church). As a result of the difficulty in getting out of Dereham, I was concerned I would miss the last bus to Thetford from Watton. We followed a tractor for over five miles and arrived just as the bus I wanted was pulling away. It really was a case of dashing across the road and flagging it down. Fortunately I just made it and would have the luxury of knowing one of a couple of buses would be available to finish my journey.

> **Alternative:** It is at moments like that when you need a plan B. All these small Norfolk towns are connected by bus with Norwich. I knew I could always rely on returning from Norwich by train or by buses to Diss and then to Bury

The 81 route to Theford from Watton is lovely. You branch off the main road at Griston, past Wayland Prison. Then it is on through the lovely villages of Griston, Caston and Great Hockham. You pass the East Wretham Nature Reserve as you head for Thetford. The bus station is beside the river and close to the Priory. As I've indicated before, Thetford has quite a lot to offer beyond the planning disaster that is the town's centre.

The day was drawing on and my last bus (route 84) was a more direct one than the 332 I had used on the previous expedition.

We positively zoomed along to Bury in under the scheduled thirty minutes. I had travelled a mighty long way and was back in Bury by five-thirty.

Expedition 30: A circular trip starting and finishing at Wells on the Norfolk Coastal route

Bus 29: Wells to Fakenham: 26 minutes
Bus 9: Fakenham to Holt: 32 minutes
Bus 46: Holt to Wells: 43 minutes

This is a truly lovely route that can be accessed from almost anywhere in North Norfolk. There are many delightful alternatives, such as this Thursday route...
Coasthopper bus from Wells to Blakeney: 19 minutes
Bus 46: Blakeney to Fakenham: 40 minutes (Thursday only)
Bus 46: Fakenham to Holt: 58 minutes
Bus 5: Holt to Sheringham: 17 minutes
Coasthopper bus from Sheringham to Wells: 43 minutes

Wells-next-the-sea is actually some distance from the sea. At the front, you look out on river and salt-marsh, though you can follow the beach road and find a sandy spot to bathe or just to lounge in the sun. You can catch the 29 bus from near the front, outside the Ark Royal, or at the top of the town at the place known as the Buttlands. If you are driving there, you can park away from the quay for nothing.

The 29 route takes you out past the newly established Eceni Centre and into the countryside in the direction of Walsingham (visited on excursion 14). Here, you through pass the historic village, close to Abbey ruins and shrines, before heading out towards Barsham and on into Fakenham.

Fakenham has a number of small antiques shops and centres. If you check out the map in the square, you can see there are several attractive walks marked starting from there. The Mill walk is lovely and is only about a mile. There are also several tea-shops.

The Bus 9 route to Holt begins by meandering around parts of Fakenham before motoring at speed towards Melton Constable. At one point, you pass fairly close to the Thursford Steam collection. After touring Briston, there is a pleasant run through wooded countryside, then in and out of Hunworth, and on into Holt.

Holt has so much to recommend it. I was glad I had allowed myself a couple of hours there. There are yet more antique centres and copious numbers of tea-rooms. I enjoyed a good lunch on the roof terrace of the restaurant attached to Bakers and Larners store.

> **Alternative:** There are two steam railways close to today's trip. The Wells-Walsingham Railway might easily be worked into the journey. Likewise, the Poppy Line from near Holt to Sheringham (a number of buses link Holt town with the station) could be a delightful addition to the plan of the day.)

Only one bus a day goes the whole way from Holt to Wells. It follows a fabulous route and was my main reason for this expedition. Almost immediately after leaving Holt, you pass Letheringsett Mill (open to the public). On the right is Bayfield Hall, with its ruined church behind it. Next come the lovely villages of Glandford and Wiveton, where the narrowest of lanes lead you into Cley. You notice the villages along this route are almost exclusively filled with typical Norfolk flint-faced cottages.

> **Alternative:** Once in Cley, you are on the Coasthopper bus route. If you prefer, you could leave the bus here and explore Cley itself - it is small, but almost everywhere you look there are places of interest. There are also the marshes, beloved by bird-watchers. The Coasthopper bus runs through here about every half hour in both directions.

I stayed with the 46 as we motored on by way of Blakeney and Morston (There are seal trips to be had here). There was then an inland stretch, where we passed through Langham and Binham, with its lovely Benedictine Priory (see picture opposite). Then it was on to Wells where the journey had all begun.

Binham Priory

Expedition 31: From Sudbury to Dunmow & Thaxted and back

Bus 12: Sudbury to Halstead: 44 minutes
Bus 21: Halstead to Braintree: 35 minutes
Bus 133: Braintree to Great Dunmow: 32 minutes
Bus 313: Great Dunmow to Thaxted: 23 minutes
Returning the same way, or by an alternative route also described.

     A volcano had erupted in Iceland, leading to all flights in and out of the U.K. being grounded. It was the best time possible to visit the attractive places blighted by Stansted's usual incessant roar.

     The route from Sudbury to Braintree was much as described in expedition 27. Approaching Braintree, you are, as I have discovered before, led into a false sense that you might get there directly when, only two miles from your destination, the bus veers off through Bocking and surrounding housing estates, taking another fifteen minutes before it finally reaches the bus station.

Braintree on a warm Saturday isn't a bad place to find yourself. The market place has a continental feel, complete with pavement cafés. I was only there a short while before boarding the 133 to Great Dunmow. Leaving Braintree, you are carried into the more rural reaches of that part of Essex. The bus reaches Dunmow by way of the attractive village of Felsted, dominated by its public school.

This bus route continues as far as Stansted Airport and a keen plane spotter might wish to continue. But the day I went, for reasons already mentioned, that was not an option.

Great Dunmow has a good collection of shops and eating places. It has a number of historic buildings and is worthy of a visit in its own right. There is a super local museum housed in some old maltings buildings.

The next leg of my journey involved a rattly bus on bumpy roads, but the views more than compensated for any discomfort. The hedgerows were ablaze with blossom and we passed a number of fine houses with equally fine gardens.

Thaxted

Thaxted is a gem of a place. The church is magnificent. It sits at the end of a narrow cobbled street called Stoney Lane, and to reach it you pass Dick Turpin's House (Well, he did come from Hempstead, just a few miles away) - pictured below. I had less than an hour to take in the atmosphere so, after sampling the bird song of the church-yard, I found a pub serving Adnams Broadside and soaked up the sunshine in their garden.

Returning the way I had come was straightforward, though I did save myself half an hour in Braintree by leaving the bus in the market place and immediately boarding the next bus bound for Halstead. I'd have missed it if I'd stayed on the bus all the way to the bus station.

You don't have to return home the same way. There are several other alternatives. From Thaxted, one possible route is...

Bus 5: Thaxted to Saffron Walden: 25 minutes
Bus 59: Saffron Walden to Haverhill: 34 minutes
Bus 345: Haverhill to Bury. St. Edmunds: 50 minutes
Bus 753: Bury St. Edmunds to Sudbury: 1 hour

I was travelling on a Saturday. Mid-week, there is the added advantage of the lovely route 236 between Haverhill and Sudbury. You might consider doing this journey in reverse, starting and finishing at Haverhill.

Expedition 32: A circular tour from Framlingham to Woodbridge and back

Bus 63: Framlingham to Woodbridge: 36 minutes
(or break the journey at Wickham Market and then continue on a 64 bus)
Bus 179: Woodbridge to Hemley corner: 19 minutes
Walk past Hemley Church and explore the creeks, returning to Newbourne (use O.S. Explorer map 197).
Bus 179: Newbourne Fox to Martlesham: 12 minutes
Bus 64 (or a number of others): Martlesham to Ipswich: 28 minutes
Bus 118: Ipswich to Framlingham: 50 minutes

This journey is particularly lovely because it takes you by way of some of the best rural routes to be found in Suffolk. Also I found, starting from Framlingham just before 10:00 a.m., you have breathing space between buses at every point - time for coffee and cake. You could easily begin and end this trip at Wickham Market instead. As with Framlingham, parking is cheap (or even free) and plentiful.

From Framlingham to Wickham Market is quick and pleasant as you follow the River Ore through Parham. I broke my journey at Wickham as I'm particularly fond of the teashop in the market square. Wickham Market is a delightful little place with a splendid church that was once reputed to have a view of nearly fifty churches from its tower.

It is only a short run to Woodbridge from there through Ufford and Melton. Time spent in Woodbridge is never wasted. There are so many nooks and crannies to explore. I always feel drawn to the water's edge. All too soon however, my 179 bus had arrived and I was on my way again. The 179 takes a long and ambling route, eventually ending in Ipswich but I asked to be dropped at the corner leading to Hemley. This is just before the road plunges down into Newbourne.

Alternative: If you leave the bus by the lane that leads to Martlesham Church, you can follow one of the abundant footpaths that take you round the woods and riverside that is Martlesham Creek.

The way I had planned it, I had a choice between walking to Waldringfield , or the other way along the river towards Kirton Creek (see O.S. Explorer map 197). Unfortunately, you can no longer reach Waldringfield along the river edge and you need to follow the lane beside the church and pick up footpaths and bridleways that take you the two miles to Waldringfield. If you are using this route, remember, the 179 bus does not come down to the river and you need to walk up as far as Mill Road to catch the next bus back.

On this occasion, I worked things a little differently. Leaving the bus, you have a half-mile walk to what amounts to the tiny hamlet of Hemley. I had barely started when a sound alerted me to an agitated oyster catcher driving off a marsh harrier from where it was nesting in a sugar-beet field.

Beside the Deben at Hemley

I opted to continue down to the marshes and along to Kirton Creek, before doubling back and cutting across to Newbourne by footpath. There was just time to visit the Fox for half a pint before my bus was due.

I had the shortest of waits before the bus arrived. That took me as far as Martlesham Water Bridge. Plenty of buses pass there on their way to Ipswich. The first to arrive was a 64. We entered Ipswich along the Rushmere Road. I got off at Tower Ramparts and stretched my legs by walking down to the bus station. I almost beat the bus there.

There are two different routes operating between Framlingham and Ipswich. The 118 route took us out along the Westerfield Road which meant we followed the edge of Christchurch Park. A sequence of villages followed. Look out for Swilland Church with what looks like a Swiss Chalet perched on its spire (pictured right).

We passed close to Otley Hall (which is open to the public on certain occasions), before heading out towards Cretingham. For some miles we saw few houses and fewer vehicles. Leaving Cretingham, we were able to look down on the full beauty of the upper Deben valley. Next

Swilland church spire

came Brandeston, an elegant village; then finally Kettleburgh where a curious notice announced 'Cow Pat Field'. I can only assume the cow inhabiting the field was called Pat.

I arrived at Framlingham in time to enjoy a final coffee and cake in the teashop nearby. What a great day!

The Great spotted woodpecker is just one of the many birds you might be fortunate enough to encounter at Wolves Wood near Hadleigh in Suffolk. You can reach this Wildlife Reserve from service 91 between Hadleigh and Hintlesham in Suffolk. The 87 & 88 from Ipswich to Stowmarket will take you close to Combs Wood. Sheringham Park in Norfolk is close to Sanders routes 4 & 5. Narborough Woods in Norfolk are a short walk from route X1 between Swaffham and Kings Lynn. On a Wednesday, the 321 passes near Bradfield Woods in Suffolk.

Ickworth Park - can be reached from service 344 & 345 buses (Bury to Haverhill)

Sail lofts at Tollesbury, Essex. Can be reached by service 95 from Maldon

Expedition 33: From Stowmarket to Coggeshall and back
(Wednesday only)

Bus 384: Stowmarket to Bury: 1 hour 10 minutes
Bus X16: Bury to Coggeshall: 1 hour 10 minutes
Bus 70: Coggeshall to Colchester: 42 minutes
Bus 93: Colchester to Ipswich: 1 hour 13 minutes
Bus 87: Ipswich to Stowmarket: 46 minutes

> Alternative: This whole expedition can be enjoyed, starting and finishing in Bury. To return from Colchester, take the 753 to Sudbury, then on to Bury (1 hour 55 minutes). It is a lovely route, but you can't hang about - the last bus leaves Colchester quite early.

Those towns that still have a regular 'market day' often attract once-a-week buses. Stowmarket and Diss are a bit like that, but best of all is Bury St. Edmunds on a Wednesday. Conveniently, most buses seem to return remarkably early, enabling the traveller to use them as a start to an afternoon's exploration.

> **Alternatives:** On Wednesdays from Bury, you could try:
> **Bus 905**: to Brinkley, followed by Bus 19 to Linton, Bus 13 to Cambridge & Bus 11 to Bury.
>
> **Bus 320**: to Finningham, Bus 456/458 to Diss & Bus 304 to Bury
>
> **...but most strongly recommended...**
> **Bus 315**: Bury to Gasthorpe; walk part of the Angles Way (2 miles) to Hopton Church bus shelter. This takes you round the lovely Hopton Fen.
> Then Bus 338 from Hopton to Bury. **(See Expedition 33A)**

This time I chose the Coggeshall link. It is interesting to note that the X16 leaves five minutes after the 753 to Sudbury, but reaches there about 15 minutes earlier, as the route is more direct. The same is true of the next part of the journey to Halstead. Where the regular service buses visit all surrounding villages, this bus stays on the main road. The two main roads used up to this point still offer attractive views. It was the end of April and in the patches of woodland we passed, bluebells were just beginning to assert themselves.

We motored on through Earls Colne to Coggeshall. Not long ago, this used to be filled with antique shops, but more recently, these have gradually disappeared. One survivor I located near the centre

was dark and had a 'back in 5 minutes' note in the window. I was there an hour, during which time nothing changed.

There are two fine National Trust properties in Coggeshall; Paycocke's and the Grange Barn. Paycocke's (see below) in particular is well worth a visit; being a sixteenth century merchant's house close to the

market-place and full of elaborate woodcarving and fine old panelling.

From Coggeshall, the journey towards Colchester is generally unspectacular, but it is worth mentioning that you pass close to Copford Church (see www.copfordchurch.org.uk), widely regarded as one of the most beautiful in Essex. In Colchester, you may have a short wait for your next bus.

The 93 bus from Colchester to Ipswich is another of those that visits a host of villages on both sides of the most direct route. Still, it can be a pleasant trundle through Stratford St. Mary, East Bergholt, Great Wenham and Washbrook.

Then it was straight off one bus and onto another, returning to Stowmarket through Claydon and Needham Market.

Expedition 33A: From Bury St. Edmunds to Gasthorpe and back (Wednesday only)

Bus 315: Bury to Gasthorpe: 46 minutes
Walk part of the Angles Way (2 miles) to Hopton (OS map 230)
Bus 338: Hopton to Bury: 49 minutes

Like a number of once-a-week buses, the 315 visits corners neglected by the main service routes. We travelled out through Great Barton before plunging down the narrowest of roads round parts of Pakenham. We passed Pakenham Watermill (open to the public 3 days a week - not Wednesdays - for seven months of the year). Then it was on through Ixworth and Ixworth Thorpe to Bardwell. Here we passed the windmill (now undergoing an ambitious restoration programme). Once out into the countryside again, we edged towards the Breckland, skirting Knettishall Heath, then crossing the Little Ouse into the tiny village of Gasthorpe; the end of this part of the journey.

I then needed to walk east along Lodge Lane, which begins right beside where I'd been dropped. No more than a quarter of a mile along the way, I had the opportunity to deviate north a short way to visit the now derelict church of St. Nicholas (pictured right).

It seems a little sad that a building that once owed its existence to the skill and love of medieval craftsmen should be laid low like this, but it is still a mystical spot to visit.

Once back to the lane, signs for the 'Angles Way' footpath, lead you the rest of the way to Hopton. Midway through your walk, you can pause and explore Hopton Fen, a rather lovely wetland Nature Reserve. Reed warblers and sedge warblers could be heard and the fields around rang with skylark song. It was a hot day and I was glad to find Hopton has a good shop selling, amongst other things, ice-cold drinks.

I had only a short wait before my 338 bus arrived, bang on time to return me to Bury. Again, this involved a lovely ride around Market Weston and Coney Weston, Barningham and Hepworth.

Expedition 34: From Beccles to Blythburgh and Southwold
(Tuesday & Friday only)

Bus 536: Beccles to Blythburgh: 50 minutes
Bus 520: Blythburgh to Southwold: 11 minutes
Bus 523 or 524: Southwold to Beccles: about 40 minutes

The 536 bus runs twice a week from Walberswick to Beccles and back. It returns in the early afternoon, which is when I caught it from the old market place in Beccles. If you are driving to Beccles, you can find free parking just ten minutes walk away, down at the quay.

The route to Blythburgh is devious and lovely. On leaving Beccles, you soon plunge

into the back of beyond, through *Weston, Sotterley* and *Brampton*. By and by, you reach *Blyford*, before moving on through *Wenhaston* to *Blythburgh*.

> **Alternative:** Leaving the bus at Blyford Queen's Head, you can pick up the footpath a short distance away that will enable you, by reference to O.S. Explorer map 231, to walk along the River Blyth to Blythburgh. There are several buses you may catch from there.

At Blythburgh, I had a choice. The White Hart Inn offers good refreshment. It backs on to the river and you can eat and drink with fabulous views from the beer garden. There is also the opportunity to begin a walk from here that can take you along the tidal marshes of the Blyth as far as *Walberswick* or (crossing the river by bridge) to *Southwold* (where buses can be caught).

©Richard Weale Wildlife Photography

Wood Sandpiper

As regards *Blythburgh* itself, the church is well worth a visit. You have a choice of buses to catch next. The 520 runs several times a day. You need to find the bus-shelter closest to the church on the main road. Alternatively, mid-afternoon on schooldays, the 601A can be caught from a point 15 minutes walk away, adjacent to *Henham* woods (see www.traveline.org for details).

My trip to Southwold on the 520 was short. Before I knew it, I was there. Southwold is a busy and rather lovely seaside town with much to recommend it. In and out of season, there is plenty to investigate. The new pier to the north and the harbour to the south are both a short distance away. The restored 'Electric Picture Palace' is a bit special. There is a lighthouse, a fine church and you can even take a boat trip on the 'Coastal Voyager.' Failing that, just wander up to Gun Hill (pictured below) and enjoy the sea air.

Southwold

The final leg of my bus journey involved another rural ramble around the villages of North-East Suffolk. I travelled on the 523 whereby you pass the lovely thatched church at Henstead and enter Beccles by way of the Heliport at Ellough. The 524 passes through much of the territory I had enjoyed on my way to Blythburgh. I was the last on the bus for the second half of the journey and was dropped off close to where I had parked my car. There was still time to enjoy a leisurely stroll around the quay area before heading home.

Expedition 35: From Diss to Happisburgh and back

Bus 580: Diss to Ditchingham: 58 minutes
Bus 588: Ditchingham to Norwich: 28 minutes
Bus 12A: Norwich to Stalham: 1 hour 2 minutes
Bus 34: Stalham to Happisburgh: 28 minutes
(or Bus 36 from Norwich to Wroxham: 33 minutes, and Bus 36 from Wroxham to Happisburgh: 67 minutes
Bus 34: Happisburgh to North Walsham: 16 minutes
Bus 55: North Walsham to Norwich: 39 minutes
Train from Norwich to Diss: 15 minutes

Using a combination of train journeys and bus-pass trips you can cover a lot of ground in a day. Rather than travel exactly as described above, I bought a cheap off-peak return rail ticket from Stowmarket and arrived in Norwich just before midday. If I'd rushed, I could probably have caught an earlier 12A bus to Stalham, but being relaxed is what days like this are about, so I ambled up towards Tombland and the Cathedral before making for my bus stop on Castle Meadow.

I love the way so much of Norwich's history is outlined on tablets attached to walls, telling you about places that once stood there, and even details like where sedan chairs could once have been hired.

The 12/12A buses to Stalham run severel times a day. My bus eased its way out of the city by way of Thorpe St. Andrew where the River Yare runs close by.   It seems that nearly every building down there is a pub offering food. Several have river frontage.

Once out into the country, it isn't long before you are in Broadland. Leaving Rackheath, the bus plunges down the quaintly named 'Thieves Lane' (light traffic only), and enters Salhouse village.

Alternative: At this point, you are only about a mile and a half from Salhouse Broad, one of the loveliest and least commercialised parts of the Broads. You might choose to make this your target for the day. Refer to O.S. Explorer map OL40.

One rather aggressive Broadland tufted duck

The bus carries on past Salhouse church and on to Wroxham. (described earlier in expedition 4) Beyond there, the route is via Hoveton and Horning.

Don't be surprised if you don't see much of the Broads. That is the way of things round here. Only when the roads cross rivers at places like Wroxham and later at Ludham Bridge are you aware of quite where you are. To explore the Broads, you need to leave the bus and take to Shanks' Pony.

Alternatives: Just beyond Wroxham, at Hoveton is the appropriately named Bewilderwood Adventure Park, a great place to explore. (see www.BeWILDerwood.co.uk)
There is also Hoveton Hall, whose lovely lakeside gardens are open most of thesummer. (see www.hovetonhallgardens.co.uk)
But if the Broads is what you are looking for, you can leave the bus at Horning and walk the two hundred yards or so to the place from which boats regularly sail.

I stayed with the bus as we swept on over Ludham Bridge (cycle and boat hire avilable here) and through Catfield and Sutton to Stalham.

Alternatives: At Catfield, you are only about a mile and a half from Hickling, one of the loveliest of the Broads, where the Pleasure Boat Inn sits almost surrounded by water. This is a walk worth making. At Sutton and Stalham, it's surprising how close you are to the Staithes, yet don't catch sight of the water, unless you take a short walk.

If you plan your bus journeys by reference to www.traveline.org.uk, you'll discover you have a short walk, calculated at ten minutes, to bring you to the bus stop adjacent to Tesco's on the A149. Don't panic. It takes most people no more than five minutes.

> **Alternative:** At the beginning, I suggested the possibility of using the Neaves buses numbered 36. You can pick up the second of these at Wroxham or at Stalham. This bus, in fact, follows a more attractive route from Wroxham via the Broadland villages of Neatishead and Barton Turf. It then travels to Happisburgh by way of Hickling and Sea Palling, a rather nicer route. However, if as is often the case, you are the only one on the bus, the driver may miss out some of these.

The 34 bus to Happisburgh, (on its way to North Walsham) after leaving Stalham, passes through Lessingham, with its lovely thatched church, set amidst fields. You spot the church tower and lighthouse at Happisburgh from a long way off (both are open on occasions to those who wish to view the coast from the highest points around). But you don't catch sight of the sea from the bus. You have to walk from where you are dropped, near Hill House, the only pub in the village, to the beach road. Along here people live a perilous existence, waiting for their properties to be claimed by the sea. You can see coastal erosion at its fiercest here.

I chose to return by way of North Walsham. This is an ambling route that follows one of the wildest parts of the Norfolk coast. Look out for the historic village of Paston, the ruins of Broomholm Priory at Bacton, and more more evidence of coastal erosion at Mundesley.

The second time I tried this route, the afternoon 34 bus had made Happisburgh a request-only stop. You may need to check when visiting Happisburgh that Sanders Coaches are able to guarantee you'll be able to leave before the following morning.

The final bus trip, I had covered before (see expedition 1), though following a slightly different route. I arrived back to chaos in Norwich. Having won the league, the football team were being paraded round town on an open-topped bus. I was glad to find the station and leave them to it.

Expedition 36: From East Harling to Norwich and Coltishall (Schooldays only)

Bus 10A: East Harling to Norwich: 1 hour 20 minutes
Bus 55: Norwich to Coltishall: 24 minutes
Bus 55: Coltishall to Norwich: 24 minutes
Bus 1: Norwich to Diss: 1 hour 6 minutes
Bus 371: Diss to East Harling: 30 minutes

South Norfolk has a collection of large villages (almost small towns) that are well worth seeing. This remarkably convoluted route visits a number of them. East Harling is a delightful place. I drove there and parked in the old market place. There are a few shops in the centre of East Harling today, but it obviously had a lot more in the past. Old shop windows are clearly visible at the front of what are now houses.

The bus left on time. There weren't many of us aboard to begin with, but it would be a full bus that finally entered Norwich. Kenninghall, Banham, Old and New Buckenham are fine villages with a good deal of history attached to them all. The Buckenhams both have lovely village greens. Old Buckenham claims to have the largest one in England. You may catch sight of the recently restored windmill. New Buckenham has a ruined castle and a fine old Market Cross.

> **Alternative:** Banham Zoo entrance is on this route. There are three returning buses a day, enabling you to stay as long as you choose.

Eventually, we reached Norwich. There is so much to see there that it would take a book of its own to describe the range of possibilities. I recommend you pick up the leaflet called 'Norwich 12' which guides you through a dozen of the most important historic buildings.

I moved on to Coltishall. The 55 bus to North Walsham delivers you there quickly and efficiently. There isn't that much to Coltishall. It is a pleasant enough village at the very edge of Broadland. But it has lovely river walks along the River Bure. Somewhat out of the village is a railway station on the Wroxham to Aylsham Bure Valley line (see expedition 4)

Returning to Norwich, I had a choice as to how I might return. I could catch the same bus back. There are three returning buses daily. I chose to go first to Diss. Bus 1 makes for Long Stratton, then meanders through a number of small villages such as Gissing and Burston.

Get off the Bus at Mount Pleasant. Then you'll know where to catch the last bus of the day. You'll have a little time to explore Diss. The bookshop serves coffee and cake with a splendid view of the mere.

The 371 runs on school days only. That tells you that it is likely to be full of schoolchildren. But it is a regular service bus and will convey you via Banham and Kenninghall back to East Harling.

Expedition 37: From Stowmarket to Shotley on a Sunday

Bus 88B (or 87B): Stowmarket to Ipswich: 41 minutes
Bus 98: Ipswich to Shotley: 34 minutes
Bus 202: Shotley to Ipswich: 29 minutes
Bus 88B: Ipswich to Stowmarket: 41 minutes

In East Anglia, you'll find far fewer buses running on Sundays, but a reduced service operates on a number of routes. Some of the routes are rather different on a Sunday from the rest of the week. This is so with the 88B. Starting by visiting most parts of Stowmarket, this 2-hourly service reaches Ipswich by way of Needham Market, Claydon, Bramford and Sproughton; a quick and enjoyable journey, offering the chance to get off and walk one of a number of sections of the Gipping Valley Walk (see O.S. Explorer maps 211 & 197).

The two services to Shotley alternate, enabling you to travel by one route (The 98 goes via Holbrook & Harkstead), returning later by another (The 202 goes through Chelmondiston & Woolverstone).

The 98 route takes you under the Orwell Bridge and along the river. After that, the route seems to be marked by pubs. Passing the Freston Boot, you turn towards the Compasses at Holbrook.

Orwell Bridge

Then, you plunge down through Lower Holbrook towards the Bakers Arms at Harkstead. The road is never very far from the River Stour and there are lovely walks down to and along the river.

> **Alternative:** Instead of carrying on all the way to Shotley, you might leave the bus at Erwarton church and follow the marked footpath beside the churchyard to the river, and walk the two miles to Shotley.

Sunday buses are even more reliable than those on other days - they nearly always run to time. There's no reason why they shouldn't - there's less traffic to get in the way. Along the road from Harkstead to Shotley, there's not much room for other traffic. The road is a narrow roller-coaster, It's a desperately tiny road requiring occasional evasive action at sight of any other vehicle. But it is beautiful. Eventually, you catch sight of Harwich on one side, followed by Felixstowe docks on the other. The bus runs right down along the shore to the Marina. The sun even came out for us.

Shotley Marina viewed from river level

Here, from May to the end of September, you can catch the foot-ferry to Harwich. Your bus-pass may get you a reduction in the fare. From Harwich, you can move on to Colchester, Manningtree or further along the coast to Clacton by bus. Unfortunately, no routes operate on a Sunday between Ipswich and Colchester, so if you want to try circling back this way on a Sunday, you'll need to use a train.

The 202 route from Shotley to Ipswich is slightly quicker, but less spectacular. Again there are opportunities to leave the bus and walk one of the sections along the Orwell. There are lovely riverside walks around Woolverstone and Pin Mill and views of Freston Tower to enjoy. Finally, you enter Ipswich as you left it, sweeping in under the Orwell Bridge and up towards the Docks. I stopped for a pint at the Steamboat Tavern before walking back to the bus-station.

> **Alternative:** Don't forget what a great place Dockland Ipswich is becoming. There are plenty of places to eat and drink. There is so much to see there, and river trips for those like myself who just love to be on the water.

I then returned to Stowmarket bang on time. It's good to know there are pleasant trips to be had with a bus-pass, seven days a week.

Expedition 38: A trip around Bawdsey using a dial-up bus

Bus 173: Martlesham to Felixstowe Ferry: 45 minutes
Ferry across the mouth of the Deben
Dial-up bus: Bawdsey to Woodbridge: 30 minutes
Bus 70: Woodbridge to Martlesham: 5 minutes

Increasingly, rural areas are experimenting with ways to offer more flexible forms of transport. One answer is the dial-up bus. Once a service ran from Bawdsey to Woodbridge. Now you phone 0845 604 1802 and ask for a minibus to carry you around the Hollesley - Sutton - Butley - Bawdsey area. I rang at 8:45 a.m. on the day I wanted a ride, though a day's notice is a better idea.

From Martlesham, just outside Woodbridge, I caught the 173. After circling around Martlesham Heath for a short while, we motored on through Brightwell and Kirton, ending up in Felixstowe - well, not quite ending up as this bus then continues as far as

Felixstowe Ferry.   I had allowed half an hour to cross the River Deben, which was plenty of time.   The foot ferry operates daily during the May-October period.

Alternative: If you allow yourself a bit more time, you can arrange a short river trip.   Ring the Harbourmaster on 07803 476621 or 01394 270106 to arrange it.

Bawdsey Manor

The dial-up bus arrived bang on time and full of passengers bound for Bawdsey Quay. The system seems to work well. I had asked to be taken all the way back to Woodbridge, but I might easily have made for Butley or Hollesley and returned aboard a service 71 bus.

The great advantage of the dial-up bus is that it can include places otherwise left out of regular service routes. I gather a popular destination among the bird-watching fraternity is Shingle Street, now available on demand.

We took a direct but attractive route back via Shottisham and Sutton Heath and I arrived at Woodbridge just in time to hop aboard a bus to Martlesham.

Expedition 39: Norwich to Castle Acre and back

I bought a return rail ticket from Stowmarket to Norwich: then...
Bus 6: Norwich to Watton: 1 hour 5 minutes
Bus 11: Watton to Swaffham: 37 minutes
Bus 32: Swaffham to Castle Acre: 10 minutes
Walk approximately 4 miles from Castle Acre to Narborough
        along the Nar Valley Way
Bus X1: Narborough to Norwich: 1 hour 26 minutes
Returning to Stowmarket by rail

As I've done before, I used a rail journey as part of the plan. As you will see, that makes this trip achievable from almost anywhere in East Anglia.   As I near the end of this book, I would consider this day out as one of the most delightful of all my bus excursions.

Arriving early in Norwich, I had plenty of time to amble up from the rail-station to the bus-station.   The journey from Norwich to Watton is pleasant enough. You leave the city by way of tree-lined roads and make first for the town of Wymondham. Here is a place you might well stop for a few hours. There is an old abbey, the Bridewell Museum, a fine Market Cross and riverside walks amongst the attractions.

From there you motor on through Hingham, with its elegant greens, finally arriving at Watton. I had only a short wait before my next bus (11) arrived. The route led out through Ashill, past a cluster of wind turbines. There was little wind that day and not much seemed to be happening. Then, circling round by Sporle, we entered Swaffham by way of the Ecotech Centre (open to visitors).

There was an hour or so before my next bus, so there was time for an early lunch. There is no shortage of eating places in Swaffham.

The next stage of the trip involved a ten minute bus-ride The 32 is an infrequent bus

Swaffham

that enables you to reach one of the most remarkable of Norfolk villages. The car driver can enter through a medieval gateway. The bus, I am afraid had to circle around and take a more cautious route before leaving me close to both the castle and the priory.

Castle Acre Priory

I recommend allowing time to wander around Castle Acre. It is a real gem, and worthy of more attention than I gave it that day. The Ostrich serves splendid meals and a good choice of real ales.

The castle at Castle Acre

I was keen to continue with my walk. The good thing about this excursion is that the X1 bus and the train with which I was to end the day both run quite late. So I didn't need to hurry.

Ordnance Survey Explorer map 236 clearly marks the Nar Valley Way. Added to that there are frequent signs that help you find your way through the wooded sections. The whole walk is about 4 miles but it does have the compensation of an oasis mid-way - The Stag Inn at West Acre appears when you most need it. Having walked beside and even across the River Nar, through wood and across common, a little moisture on the palate is more than welcome.

Then there are the Bradmoor Woods to negotiate. There are surprises round every corner. At one point you come across a folly buried at the back of a clearing. Squirrels and woodpeckers, herons and warblers frequent this woodland. You are never far from the river, or from Narford Lake.

The folly in the woods near Narborough

Eventually, you reach a series of fishing lakes and cross the A47 before entering Narborough. You need to walk to the cross-roads at the centre of Narborough as that is the only place the X1 will stop. There is a bench conveniently placed, from which you can see when the bus is coming.

The final part of the bus journey meant drifting in and out of Dereham before making for the road to Norwich, and the bus station where I had started several hours before.

Alternative: The North Norfolk Railway runs between two places on this excursion - Wymondham and Dereham (and hopes eventually to run as far as Fakenham). It operates at weekends throughout much of the year and on other days during the summer season. With a bit of forward planning, a steam rail journey might be incorporated in a trip like this (see www.mnr.org.uk)

I'd had enough of walking and caught a bus from the adjacent St. Stevens Street to the railway station. I hopped straight onto a train bound for home.

There is something in this trip for everybody - history, natural history, good food and drink, glorious views... oh, and some really enjoyable bus travel.

Expedition 40: A mammoth circular trek to Peterborough and beyond

Bus 12: Newmarket to Ely: 45 minutes
Bus X9: Ely to March: 61 minutes
Bus 33: March to Peterborough: 57 minutes
Bus X4: Peterborough to Oundle: 22 minutes
Bus X4: Oundle to Kettering: 54 minutes
Bus M50: Kettering to Bedford: 1 hour 22 minutes
Bus X5: Bedford to Cambridge: 1 hour 10 minutes
Bus 11 or 12: Cambridge to Newmarket: 48 minutes

You can travel a very long way in a day as this trip seeks to demonstrate. Whilst it may not be everyone's cup of tea to spend this much time on buses, I was keen to show where your bus travels might lead you.

I began at Newmarket, where it is not too difficult to park for nothing all day within easy reach of the bus-station. The trip to Ely is pleasant enough once you get out of Newmarket. Ely itself is well worth a longer look. It is neat and compact with a wonderful cathedral amongst its many attractions. On this occasion there was no time for sightseeing as I stepped off one bus and onto another, an X9, bound for March.

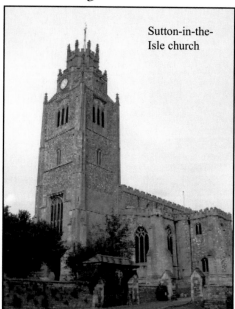

Sutton-in-the-Isle church

The fens being what they are, you spot landmarks from a long way off. St. Andrew's Church at Sutton-in-the-Isle stands out above the surrounding flat land, looking much like a pepperpot. March is arrived at after further treks through the fens. This is a busy little place that seems to have railways pointing in all directions from it.

Having crossed a number of railway tracks, we journeyed on past rivers and dykes and wind-turbines, beside fields that sat well below the river-banks, and with soil as black as your hat. Whittlesey is worth a mention. Easily the most attractive of the fenland towns, it is worthy of further inspection if you have the time. With more than its fair share of ancient buildings and the unusual thatched clay-lump walls around a number of properties, Whittlesey is a place to explore.

Unfortunately, I had longer distances to cover. We soon reached Peterborough which was entered (and left behind) remarkably quickly. The brickyard chimneys greet you as you enter the city. The bus station is modern and easy to find your way around. It is close to shops and tourist attractions. Though not the prettiest of cities, Peterborough has enough attractions to fill a number of days. It has a fine cathedral and any number of museums and galleries. There is a riverside area beside the River Nene and you are close to other places of interest.

Alternatives: You are not far from the lovely old town of Stamford, reachable by bus routes 9, 201 or 4P. The 201 passes right past the gates to Burghley House. From the Bus station, you are within easy walking distance of the Nene Valley Railway, which runs to Wansford and back throughout much of the year.

The kind of surprise bus journeys can spring on you - a field filled with rosebay willow-herb

The X4 runs hourly and links Peterborough with Corby, Kettering, Wellingborough, Northampton and Milton Keynes. To begin with, we climbed away from the fens past Warmington (not '-on-sea') and on to the town of Oundle. If anyone should attempt this expedition and is seeking a place to rest awhile, Oundle is definitely the place to choose. It is a lovely stone town, full of fascinating buildings, tea-rooms and hidden corners. It is everything that Corby is not. We reached Corby after entering a much bendier and more rural piece of England. I saw a sparrowhawk, a hobby and two herons from that bus. Corby is a town that has been forced to re-invent itself and is still in the process. I do like the way the bus and train stations sit side by side, almost sharing a platform.

From there, it was on to Kettering and a short break before catching an M50 bus to Bedford. This route passed some places of interest. Look out for what appears at first to be an octagonal church tower at Finedon. It turns out to be a rather unusual water-tower. At Felmersham and Radwell you enter what is almost an island encircled by the River Ouse. High raised walkways are visible at entry and exit to the villages. Flooding here is common.

At Bedford, I had a short wait for the X5, a luxury coach that runs between Cambridge and Oxford almost every half hour, seven days a week (see expedition 11). This leg of the journey was fast and comfortable and brought me in to Cambridge in plenty of time to catch a bus back to Newmarket. On the day in question, the X5 terminated about 500 yards from the bus station. This varies from time to time, and if you know Cambridge, it may be worthwhile getting off sooner and walking through the town. To reach Newmarket, either the 11 or 12 will do, whichever comes first. We finally entered Newmarket as darkness fell. I was the last person remaining on the bus.

Last bus home

Santon Downham - the grass snake picture inserted was taken there. This idylic spot is close to route 201 between Brandon & Thetford

A typical Norfolk Broadland scene. Take a 108 from Lowestoft to Oulton Broad or a Bus 6 from Great Yarmouth to Potter Heigham or a service 12 from Norwich to Salhouse.

Useful phone numbers and websites

www.traveline.org.uk
or www.traveline.info

www.cambridgeshire.gov.uk/transport
www.essexcc.gov.uk
www.norfolk.gov.uk/travel_and_transport
www.suffolkonboard.com

Dial-a-ride buses - These operate in different ways in different counties. In some cases, community and dial-up services are restricted to certain groups, such as the disabled. However, in some rural areas, they offer an alternative to regular service buses and are available to all...

Norfolk Flexibus (North Walsham Area) 01692 500840
Norfolk Flexibus (Acle Are) 01493 752223
Norfolk Flexibus (Wayland area) 0845 600 2315
Norfolk Flexibus (Wymondham area) 0845 600 2315
Norfolk Brecks bus (Breckland area) 01638 608080
Borderhoppa: (Diss and North Suffolk) 01379 854800

Suffolk demand responsive transport:
Cosford area (Bildeston, Lavenham area): 01473 826242
Gipping area (Stowmarket, Needham Mkt. area): 01449 616000
Three towns (Haverhill, Newmarket, Clare area): 0845 604 1802
Wilford area (Bawdsey to Orford area): 0845 604 1802

These may have the added advantage of taking you to places that never had a bus service before. Birdwatchers regularly use the Wilford area service to explore the Shingle Street/Hollesley area of the Suffolk coast.

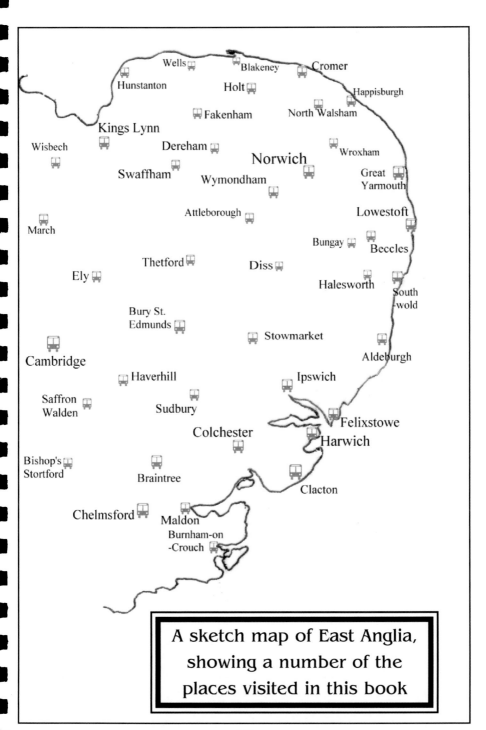

Wells
Blakeney
Cromer
Hunstanton
Holt
Happisburgh
Fakenham
North Walsham
Kings Lynn
Wisbech
Dereham
Wroxham
Norwich
Swaffham
Great
Wymondham
Yarmouth
Attleborough
Lowestoft
March
Bungay
Beccles
Thetford
Diss
Ely
Halesworth
South
-wold
Bury St.
Edmunds
Stowmarket
Cambridge
Aldeburgh
Haverhill
Ipswich
Saffron
Walden
Sudbury
Felixstowe
Colchester
Harwich
Bishop's
Stortford
Braintree
Clacton
Chelmsford
Maldon
Burnham-on
-Crouch

A sketch map of East Anglia, showing a number of the places visited in this book

Thanks are owed to Will Black (www.willblack.co.uk) for the use of three photographs in this book. Also thanks to Richard Weale, wildlife photographer, for the inclusion of two of his bird pictures.

Thanks to Poppyland Publishing for the use of the Cromer picture on page 31. Final thanks to the Public Transport Departments of Norfolk and Suffolk County Councils for their support and encouragement in the publishing of this book.

©Will Black Photography